7

WITHDRAWN

God's Water Carriers

All Our Yesterdays

God's Water Carriers

Manès Sperber

*Translated from the German
by Joachim Neugroschel*

With a foreword
by Elie Wiesel

HOLMES & MEIER
New York | London

Holmes & Meier Publishers, Inc.
30 Irving Place
New York, NY 10003

Great Britain:
1–3 Winton Close
Letchworth, Hertfordshire SG61 1BA
England

Book design by Mark O'Connor

Originally published in German under the title *Die Wasserträger Gottes*
by Europa Verlag 1974 as volume 1 of the trilogy *All das Vergangene*.
Copyright © Mrs. Zenija Sperber.

Library of Congress Cataloging-in-Publication Data

Sperber, Manès, 1905–
   God's water carriers.

   (All our yesterdays ; v. 1)
   Translation of: Die Wasserträger Gottes.
   1. Sperber, Manès, 1905–   —Biography.
2. Authors, German—20th century—Biography.
I. Neugroschel, Joachim. II. Title. III. Series:
Sperber, Manès, 1905–   . All das Vergangene.
English ; v. 1.
PT2639.P47Z47713   1987   833'.914   [B]   87-21230
ISBN 0-8419-1031-6 (alk. paper)

This book has been printed on acid-free paper.
Manufactured in the United States of America

And all our yesterdays have lighted fools
The way to dusty death.

—William Shakespeare

CONTENTS

FOREWORD

Elie Wiesel

I would have liked to write this preface as a letter. A letter to Manès Sperber. To tell him that I miss him. That I need his presence, his wisdom, his strength of character that had a touch of moving tenderness. I need his exigent vision as much as I need his sense of humor. I need his advice, his criticism, his *Mussar*,* just as much as I need his friendship; in short, I need to think of him, to imagine him alive. But I know him; he would laugh at me; he would make a little gesture with his hand as though to warn me: "You and your Narishkeiten,† you old Hasid. How many times do I have to tell you there's no life after death?" But he's wrong. It turns out that even he can be wrong: death does not end the life of a man, certainly not a man and a writer like him. Manès, my friend Manès, is alive, for his work means a refusal of death. No, Manès will not die, nor will the admiration of his readers who need his voice, his words, in order not to die.

Our first meeting was connected to the fate of Soviet Jews. A coincidence? Jewish history denies coincidence. Let us say rather that it was symbolic. It was Jewish suffering, or the suffering of distant Jews, that brought us together.

Brussels, 1964. Manès delivered a speech at a conference on the fate of Soviet Jewry. The audience was large and attentive. Manès knew how to interest and stimulate. Lucid, erudite, he presented the facts and allowed you the task of drawing the conclusion that amounted to a call

*ethical teachings
†foolishness

for action. Because of its ethical rigor and its Judaic dimension, his speech could not fail to impress me. It made me want to know the man.

I knew his work. His trilogy will remain one of the indispensable witnesses to the ideological and political turbulences of our century. Everything is there: nostalgia for justice, passion for humanity, profound love for the Jewish people. Nothing is treated superficially. There are no wasted words, no obvious scenes. Attracted by the depths of creatures with a dark destiny, he chose a pure, spare style. His characters, full of sorrowful intensity, are striking by their exemplary nature. They all seem to be true to life: the communists just as much as the pious Jews. He speaks only of what he knows, what he has lived.

So, at our first meeting—arranged, if I remember correctly, by a mutual friend, the poet and journalist Michel Salomon—we talked a lot about his shtetl, Zablotow, which oddly reminded me of mine, Sighet.

I liked to hear him tell the stories and the picturesque and mysterious legends of Zablotow. It was as though he were still there, walking at ease among the unlighted cottages and through the study house where, night and day, especially on Shabbat and on the holy days, the faithful sang and prayed. Other Jewish writers have tried to describe the infinite colors of the shtetl, but none has spoken with so much authority. Nor with so much tenderness.

Of course, Manès was not religious. he declared it openly so there would be no room for misunderstanding: the future intellectual and idealist, the lover of humanity, rejected all religions, mine, ours, included. Many were the times that he criticized what he called my "Judeocentrism." In his view, I was mistaken to emphasize so heavily the role that Jewish religion played in the Jewish renaissance in the Soviet Union. According to him, it was simply a sociocultural phenomenon: all mankind deserved freedom, and Soviet Jewish man as well. He deserved to be free from any constraint, political or religious; he could and should get rid of both.

In the first volume of his autobiography, Manès tells of his first break with the community. He was still a child; he attended *cheder* and synagogue; listening to the kaddish of orphans, he was both moved and disturbed. How long, he wondered, would God allow death to carry off men in order to hear the song of their children praising His glory, His mercy? Of course, when questions remain unanswered, there's faith. But Manès, rationalist through and through, mistrusted a faith that blinded rather than enlightened. If he joined the Revolution, this was because at the beginning it took the place of faith. Ten years later, he left the Communist Party because he considered communism a new faith. It was the time of the show trials. In Moscow, Lenin's former comrades were accusing each other of every sin on earth. European intellectuals in general disapproved of these trials but accepted them. Not Manès. As for Manès, he rejected all prisons; those built for men and those invented for their thoughts. Manès wanted to be a free man. All his work testifies to this fact.

And yet, despite his protestations and denials, he remained rooted in the religious culture of our people. He adored Yiddish literature, and his adoration was contagious. He never succeeded in freeing himself from the enchantment, if not the influence, of Hasidic tales. In New York, in the 1960s, I took him to a celebration held by the Lubavitch Rabbi. Manès was happy. We were elbowed and jostled by the crowd, but Manès did not complain. He was happy, I tell you. Happy to be in the midst of Hasidim. Happy to see himself again as a child in Zablotow. I introduced him to the Rabbi, who asked him about his origins and his work. Manès answered in Yiddish. Manès was radiant. He was in his element. But the exaggerated attachment of the disciples to their Master? But faith in God? But "Judeocentrism"? Manès would criticize them. For the moment, he was with the crowd that was vibrant with fervor and hope. After all, what was Lubavitch but a striking triumph over communist dictatorship?

Manès is authentically a Jew in this trilogy. Even when he rebels against the Jewish tradition, it is the Jew in him who rebels. And who searches for himself. And who shares.

Finally translated into English, this trilogy will make Manès known to many American readers. I envy them their joy in discovering a great writer, a marvelous teller of tales, a remarkable thinker.

I am going to reread this trilogy, and I am going to reread his novels: to rediscover him, wise and amusing, dominating and generous, as only great and true creators are.

I can see him as we last met. We were speaking of the same problems that had preoccupied us in Brussels twenty years earlier. We embraced. He was crying. I, too, felt like crying. I left him with a heavy heart.

That is why I am going to reopen his books. To hear him laugh.

Translated from the French
by George Holoch

INTRODUCTION

Werner Rings

In *God's Water Carriers,* the first volume of this autobiographical trilogy, Manès Sperber portrays the East Galician shtetl of Zablotow where he was born in 1905. Here, in a poor, ugly, often repulsive world that was centuries behind the times but which nevertheless aroused his admiration, he spent the first ten years of his life. Crowded together in a narrow space, three thousand people lived in utter poverty. Very few of them ever had enough to eat. Children went barefoot until late autumn, and in the winter some families had to make do with a single pair of boots.

Sperber describes this village, inhabited almost exclusively by Jews, a center of activity surrounded by Slavic villages. Most of those who lived outside the shtetl, hidden in the vast snowy fields during the winter, were illiterate. The shtetl, however, was filled with self-aware descendants of Abraham, literate custodians of a religious tradition that had endured centuries of dreadful persecution.

Most of them were believers in the truest sense of the word. As a child Sperber observed that for them, the excessive pain and suffering they had to endure was merely proof that the Messiah, who would redeem the world—including the citizens of Zablotow—was about to arrive. Who could doubt that the Messiah was practically at the door, that he might enter at any moment?

Sperber calls these people "permanent worshipers." "The men," he writes, "devoted the first hour of the day and one other hour, before or after the onset of evening, to prayer. The rest of the time offered countless opportunities for blessings: when we washed our hands before a meal, before we put the first bite of bread into our mouths, before we drank the first drop, when we ate the first fresh fruit of the year—there was no end of blessings.

"The kaddish, spoken by the male offspring for one year after the death of a close relative, impressed me the most." Orphan boys, including those who had only just begun to speak, were brought to the house of prayer in the morning and in the evening so that they might recite the kaddish to honor a prematurely deceased father or mother. Even seven decades later, Sperber admits that when he evokes the past, he is always overwhelmed by the emotions he felt in his boyhood when he listened to the orphan boys stammering the long prayer, faltering through it in front of the mute worshipers.

In a milieu of such intense, all-pervasive faith, completely ruled by religious "shalts" and "shalt-nots" that everyone took for granted, Sperber, the boy, could scarcely imagine that Jews might live any other way. His religious training had begun very early. By the time he was three, before he could even read, he was deeply shaken upon hearing the prayers and readings from the Torah on holidays. The child felt that something "tremendous" was happening. At the age of four, he began attending the *heder*, the Jewish school, where he learned to translate paragraphs, then short passages, then longer sections of the books of the Old Testament, reciting them to adults. Sperber's childhood and adolescence were filled with evocative practices of a life of devotion.

However, Sperber's intellectual and spiritual faculties were not molded solely by religious discipline. The shtetl of Zablotow was not a ghetto. That is, it was not an alien element despised by a surrounding higher civilization. It was not a neighborhood for a mistreated minority. On the contrary, it was a "sharply delineated autonomous society that rested on a solid foundation, virtually a small-scale Civitas Dei of a Jewish majority, accustomed to dealing intensely and meticulously with the spiritual." They could, not unjustifiably, assume that they were superior to others in certain ways. In any event, these Jews were in no way tempted to deny their background, their faith, or to conceal their Jewishness.

How was it possible that Sperber, while still young, managed to break out of this solid religious community? Answers to this question can be found in the trilogy. An initial doubt (Sperber calls it "a malaise") was aroused in him by the apparently senseless death of an innocent person who succumbed to an incurable disease. The survivors, whose already straitened circumstances were now worsened, had to recite the kaddish three times a day. God, the Creator, had to be praised and glorified with words that offended five-year-old Manès. Did God really need to have wretched orphans keep reiterating that He, He alone, was great and wondrous, that He alone had created the universe, that His will alone determined everything, that He alone had led the Jews from Egypt into freedom, giving them the land of Canaan for their very own? And the boy kept asking: Does God really want to force tired, sleepy orphans to keep praising him, over and over, morning, afternoon, evening, late at night?

Is God omniscient? Is God omnipotent? Doubts upon doubts. Even doubts in God's justice—but doubts that could not shake the boy's "faith in the God of our ancestors." The Messiah will come—the boy knew it—and when He does come, no one will need God's help because everything will be as good as can be. The boy frequently climbed up to the roof of the barn and hurled stones at the sky. He wanted to hit God: When God opens the trapdoor in the sky and glares down at him, the boy will reproach Him bitterly because he has been holding back the Messiah for such a long time and is still holding Him back—why?

Doubt remained a component of Manès Sperber's faith. At the age of ten, during the first year of World War I, he was frightened by the sight of bleeding soldiers. He asked himself: Where is God? What use is His omnipotence for Him, for us? In 1918, at the age of thirteen, he was in Vienna, still under the protection of his parents—yesterday they were fairly prosperous citizens in the poor shtetl, then they were suddenly impoverished war refugees in Vienna. The young Sperber was confronted with a world in upheaval that threatened to knock him off balance. At fifteen, he began to sympathize with a revolutionary movement that promised to improve both the world and mankind. He had long since escaped the domination of the pious, and their religious prescriptions and proscriptions. And now he took the step that he describes tersely: "I broke with my faith."

Can we take him at his word? Had he lost the faith and confidence with which he had waited so impatiently for the Messiah? Or had his faith found a new, equally intimate tie with the messianic role of the proletariat—one of the major theses of Marxism? In 1927, having moved to Berlin, Manès Sperber, twenty-two years old, joined the Communist

Party—only to leave it, bitterly disappointed, ten years later, during the Moscow Trials. This conflict, which was serious and significant for Sperber, occupies him in *The Unheeded Warning* and *Till Shards Are Placed upon My Eyes*, the second and third volumes of *All Our Yesterdays*.

The enigma of this interlude in the life of a gifted, self-critical analyst is cleared up when we look to the past and note the early philosophical contradiction between Jewish and Hellenic beliefs. In the pre-Christian world of Greece, human life was controlled by fate. A man's destiny was preordained. No personal achievement, no loyalty, no courage or regret could change the predetermined course of things.

The Jewish prophets, however, had an entirely different view. For them, there was only one God, and He participated actively in anything that human beings did and thought. He punished those who scorned divine commandments or flouted divine will. However, God could at any time revoke His own judgment because the believer had it in his power to regret his thoughts and deeds. Indeed, he could move God to forgive him if he made the proper effort. In this regard, human conduct was considered more influential in the scheme of things than it was by the Greeks.

A sort of compromise between Jewish and Hellenic positions was reached by Marxist theory in the nineteenth century. The extraordinary appeal that Marxism had for Sperber was probably due in part to its elements of Jewish thought. On the one hand, it takes for granted the eventual self-destruction of capitalism and the messianic mission of the proletariat, as if both were preordained. But on the other hand, Marxism claims that history develops not according to the dictates of destiny, but dialectically, from one contradiction to the next, and that history, impelled by revolutionary movements, is ultimately a human creation. Sperber explains that no idea has ever so overwhelmed him and so influenced the choice of his path as the idea that the world cannot remain as it is, that it can become something completely different, and that it *will* become something completely different. Sperber presents this idea in terms of a secular Judaism as the basis for a high moral obligation that is simultaneously a social ethos.

Sperber knew that the essence of this secular—as well as traditional—Judaism could not be fully explained or defined. On the one hand, being a Jew could be interpreted as an act of free will. After all, someone born a Jew could embrace Judaism or leave it, just as a Protestant or Catholic could leave the Church. On the other hand, he also knew that renouncing the Jewish religion did not cancel out one's Jewish background. Nor did it prevent others from stamping him, the *juif déjudaisé*, a Jew without Judaism, until the end of his life. This blend of freedom and destiny appeared to be a specific existential characteristic of Judaism. For Sperber, although he was an atheist, Judaism was a mysterious legacy that required certain obligations.

What was this legacy? As he knew, during the first thousand years of Christian history, and even earlier, there were Jewish communities scattered far and wide across the Mediterranean countries; but these were converts to Judaism, and their biological lineage did not go back to Palestine. Sperber wondered: Are the Jews a nation? They lack the characteristics that one normally assigns to the idea of "nation." Jews live in larger and smaller communities scattered through disparate worlds, in Christian and in Moslem countries, in Eastern and Western Europe, in the age of Enlightenment and in the century of the Holocaust. What tied them together? No common language, no specific political system and constitution, no discernible common civilization that could be called "national," and, since the pogroms of the eleventh century, no shared destiny other than as victims of furious hatred and persecution. What then linked them beyond all vaguenesses and contradictions? Sperber saw that no one had ever managed to define the Judaism that is the prerequisite for Jewishness and concluded that Judaism could not be explained rationally.

I am returning to biography when I now discuss what was probably Sperber's worst trauma: the revelation of a lie—a lie that Sperber and countless others, in their idealistic enthusiasm, had failed to detect earlier. In the third volume of the trilogy he asks himself: Could there have been anything worse for me at that time than recognizing the Soviet-Russian perversion of the Socialist idea?

His crisis paralyzed him for many years. He maintained an angry silence and isolation. He, the "loyal heretic" (as he dubbed himself), refused to voice any public criticism of his comrades, his former party, so long as such criticism could have benefited a different source of injustice—Hitler's totalitarian state. But Stalin's alliance with Hitler allowed Sperber to speak freely. He began to write. And he found his voice in his very first books, and his voice was heard throughout and beyond the Continent.

Sperber did not follow the road taken by disillusioned Marxists who returned to religion. He remained an inveterate atheist, a provocateur of the believers: "Think of the acropolis," he once wrote: "It does not force you to believe in Zeus or Athena or any other inhabitant of Mount Olympus. Only the creative human being survives in their temples; the gods are formed in man's likeness and given existence by our perception of them."

He also prophesied that human beings will become mature only when they no longer need thunder and lightning or the vast authority of a god to behave as the Bible expects them to: when they have the courage to live without such a faith. Mournfully, perhaps silently homesick for the lost Civitas Dei of his childhood, he added: "If God existed, I am certain that He would be the Jewish God."

Because of an inner logic, the Bible maintained its central importance for Manès Sperber, the denier of God. The Jews, he says, found their homeland not in stone buildings or in idols, but in the Word. The Bible, he says, is the homeland of the Jews, and without the Bible and its promises, the Jews would have perished. He added, "The lips utter the words. When you grasp them more clearly, you know their meaning—just as a river carries other things besides water. . . . I know how deeply the Bible influences me when I write."

Sperber's legacy, according to his friend André Malraux (in Malraux's preface to Sperber's *Wolyna*), ties this agnostic, Manès Sperber, to the grandeur and darkness bequeathed by the profundity of his ideas.

Translated from the German
by Joachim Neugroschel

Werner Rings is the author of *The Disenchantment of Politics, The Enemy's Advocates, Switzerland and the War: 1933–1945,* and *Life with the Enemy, Collaboration and Resistance in Hitler's Europe 1939–1945.*

God's Water Carriers

PART ONE

God's Water Carriers

Some time ago, right after my sixtieth birthday, I realized that the face I saw in the mirror at least once a day looked completely unfamiliar. It certainly belonged to me, I carried it on my shoulders. But something had been happening to me—probably for years—and somehow, without any dramatic metamorphosis or sense of loss, my face and I had become strangers. (Since I was never handsome and had not become ugly, nothing was gained or lost.) Although my face did not belong to anyone else, it wasn't really mine, either. I have, therefore, turned my back on this face—not to escape daily disappointment or the degradation guaranteed by old age, but because I simply could not acknowledge a stranger's face as my own. And I felt no less alienated even on those occasions when I found traces of my former self in the eyes, just beneath the still dark but thinning eyebrows.

In the days that followed this ordinary and extraordinary discovery, I seriously considered writing my memoirs. Previously, I had always rejected the idea, because I deplore the way autobiographers sensationalize their own and other people's private lives. I despise the way the author's egocentricity—ranging in intensity from slight inclination to overriding compulsion—distorts complicated actions and relationships, becomes monotonous and tiresome, fraudulent, or hypochondriacal and pompous. I found it all unbearable. But it would be truly unbearable if I myself were to write memoirs. Actually, I have always been an attentive, even avid reader of the intimate literature consisting of letters, diaries, memoirs, and autobiographies. I also like to read sharp, pointed polemics; but I do not write any, nor do I much like my friends to contribute any.

It was not only this partial *disidentification*, this amazingly sober, almost unfeeling dissociation from my own face—enabling me just as soberly to distance myself from my own past—that inspired me to write my memoirs. Another factor was a minor event that lasted for only a split second. While not diminishing my qualms about the egotizing of the autobiographer, the incident did arouse something I had scarcely ever experienced: a yearning for memories. It happened in Provence under the scorching afternoon sun. I had made a long but useless effort to find Albert Camus's grave in the cemetery of Lourmarin, before we finally stopped for lunch in the village of Apt. In the streets near the large square, I looked for a restaurant but could not find one I liked. I then crossed the street in order to enter a café. Just as I was about to set foot on the sidewalk, I fell to the ground. My companion thought I had slipped, or stumbled over the curb. I was helped up, unhurt. Even the glasses in my right hand were intact because, before falling, I had raised my arm to protect them.

This basically trivial incident had considerable impact on me, for I knew I had not slipped or stumbled. For an instant, a fraction of a moment, I had simply blacked out, regaining consciousness before I hit the ground. Nothing like this had ever happened to me. It was a signal, which would not change my life in any visible way or reduce my numerous and varied activities. For many years, people like me had gone on much too long, certain that they were "living on borrowed time." But now, sitting on the café terrace and watching the bustling square, I knew that henceforth I would live in the shadow rather than in the light of that certainty. In another Provençal village, old Cagnes-sur-Mer, which had granted me comfort and refuge during the most dangerous time and the warmth and golden light of its sun on winter days, everything—my own life and that of the people closest to me—appeared before me as if I were an outside observer, registering every detail as attentively as someone who goes away and keeps looking back, knowing he will never return.

Whenever I tried to recall my earliest childhood, a snowy landscape emerged—snow on the streets and paths, on the window sills and housetops, in the back yards and the fields, on the trees, on the faraway treetops and hills. I thought I would speak about snow before anything else, about what snow has meant to me as far back as I can remember. But now, an image devoid of snow surfaces unexpectedly, as if from the

4

folds of some heavy, dusty cloth. It is late spring. The air is filled with the scent of lilac and the lure of its two colors; it blossoms on both sides of the fence separating us from the garden of our Polish neighbor. Jelena is the only Polish girl who works for us (the other girls are Ruthenians from the countryside around the Jewish shtetl); she and I climb over the fence, and she then takes me into the Polish house. She cautions me that this is to be our secret, my parents don't have to find out. Find out about what? She won't tell me, but I suspect it might have something to do with my only friend, whom I meet at the fence from time to time.

Actually, Jadzia and I scarcely knew one another. We spoke different languages, barely understanding each other, barely communicating; but that was not important. We had a rapport that involved nothing but our encounters, with each of us remaining on his or her side of the fence. In that spring, as in the previous fall, when we had first discovered each other, we were bound by a code word: *zielony*, the Polish word for "green." If either of us spoke it, then the other instantly had to produce something green: it was usually a leaf. A Jewish boy, who was almost five years old, and thus could read Hebrew fluently and was learning how to translate the weekly portion of the Torah, no longer played with girls, and certainly not with a girl belonging to the other world, the enemy world. No express prohibition prevented the children from meeting; nevertheless, they felt they had to keep their back-fence meetings a secret.

That was why I was not very surprised that the visit in Jadzia's house was to be kept secret. My parents were out of town; my brother, three years my senior, was in school. And so we headed for the house in broad daylight. I was uneasy, since this was the first time I was entering a Christian home. In the dark hall, I smelled the incense—I was familiar with it from funeral processions, and I didn't like it. The door opened; Jelena pushed me gently across the threshold, into a bright room. A tall, blond woman looked down at me, curious, severe, sad. I was frightened by her eyes, which were round and disquieting, like the eyes of a crow. She placed her hand on my shoulder and led me into the next room. Before I could enter, I looked through the open door and saw Jadzia. It was obviously she, and yet she was very different from the Jadzia I knew. She lay on a broad bed, dressed in white from head to foot, a long chain with a gold cross on her folded hands. I had never seen her hair like this: radiant blond curls framed her face, which looked older now—not a child's face.

Women in black, their heads covered with hats or veils, knelt on either side of the bed. Sometimes I stared at them and their faintly murmuring lips, sometimes at Jadzia, at her curls shining in the candle-light, and at her folded, fettered hands. I felt her mother's eyes on my face, first as a gentle then as a forceful look. I didn't know what she wanted, so I turned to Jelena, who stood behind me. She nodded at me, then knelt, pulling me down with her. It suddenly dawned on me that these Christian women wanted to trick me, a Jewish child, into commit-ting a sin. Kneeling—and before a cross, to boot—was something terri-ble, as bad as death, perhaps even worse.

I ran out and caught my breath only after I was far away from those women, behind the Ruthenian church, which concealed me from the eyes of the Poles, but also from the eyes of our servants.

I knew that people, both children and adults, died, that their bodies were washed and wrapped in white sheets before they were placed in coffins and finally buried, for in our shtetl, everything concerning death and burial was as public as the weddings. If anyone in the neighborhood died, everybody would pour all the fresh water out of buckets and basins and cover the mirrors. Anyone not kept at home by illness or urgent work would join the funeral processions, which wound through the narrow alleys and finally the main street. Thus I had often peered into the faces of corpses before they were concealed forever by the lid of a coffin. And the previous summer, on a terribly hot day, I had been in an empty shack near the river and seen the naked body of a young man who had been pulled out of the water that morning. The drowned adolescent was a stranger—that was why he lay naked on a plank; perhaps someone would recognize him. The flies buzzed around his head. One fly, always the same, perched on his eyebrows, was shooed away, and came again. I stared at it as if I had to figure out why it perched on the eyebrow; and I kept gazing at the soles of the corpse's feet, repulsed by their yellowness. This color seemed to prove that the stranger was really dead, that is, abandoned by his soul. And I would have liked to know why the soles of a departed man (that was what a dead person was for us) were yellow.

Jadzia had not looked like a corpse, she had looked like one of the young brides who were accompanied by music along the main street to the canopy, under which the groom waited. Jadzia's face had been made up, she had been dressed in a beautiful, radiant white gown, and her hands had been folded in prayer. Was she really dead? And if so, why was everyone in her home so festive? Why weren't the women wearing old, shabby clothes? Why weren't they sobbing, why weren't they praying loudly, why weren't all of them, especially the mother, seeking comfort in audible laments?

I don't remember whether I thought of Jadzia when I was alone in bed that night, whether I even felt grief. Jelena made me swear never to breathe a word about her taking me into that house, never to reveal anything to my parents or anyone else. But it is only now, as I begin this book, that the image of the dead child appears before me—her image, the abrupt ending to the scene, and the suspicion that I probably did not grieve for my dead playmate because her appearance and the conduct of the Christians made me afraid of doing so.

A day has passed since I wrote those lines. Whatever I have done since has been haunted by the suspicion that I did not say everything—that something was missing. It probably has nothing to do with other, later encounters with death, with the dreadful, murderous epidemics that were to empty so many households in our shtetl some six years later, during the war. I will talk about that later.

It concerned something very different; not death, but love. I was fifteen years old, an active member of the radical left-wing Jewish Youth Movement, which had moved its headquarters to Vienna during the world war. It was spring. Once again, we had no place to meet, no "home," as we called it; so we convened on the banks of the Danube Canal, near the Augarten Bridge. A long ramp led from this bridge down to the canal, to a grassy, gently sloping shore, that had become our "home." We could see the other members arriving as soon as they left the bridge. I was in love with a girl who often came very late, perhaps because she knew how much I looked forward to seeing her. She no longer had pigtails; her blond hair fell in curls on her shoulders, framing her full cheeks. One summery afternoon in May, I caught sight of her on the ramp as she descended slowly, too slowly. Her hair shone in the sun, she herself shone, for she was dressed in white from head to foot. As I watched her approaching, I was happy and excited, when something senseless and incomprehensible, occurred. My eyes filled with tears, I felt as if I had to sob. I had to dry my eyes quickly, quell my absurdly deep emotion before I greeted her. Perhaps that was why I didn't instantly seek a reason for my strange reaction. Not then, not later—not until this moment, half a century too late. And only now do I understand why my relationship to A. kept breaking off and resuming until we were separated by her return to Poland. Now I understand why our relationship could never be consummated, even though we desired one another and had no moral qualms about it. It was my fault; today I am more certain of this than ever.

"I've always looked forward to snow because I've yearned for purity," says a Pole in one of my novels. He says it to his girlfriend when he pulls her out of bed early one morning to show her a boulevard covered with snow. "The snow fell densely, in huge flakes. Everything was so silent that one could almost hear a very faint sigh as the snow settled on the earth." Yes, I believed it. I maintained that my earliest memories begin with that faint sigh of the falling snow.

Often, when both my father and I awoke early, he would place me in an adjustable high chair at the window, which was covered with frost flowers. The sight of them delighted me; I was so happy that I would clap my hands when I spotted them again in the morning. Nevertheless, my father would thaw some of the flowers and wipe them away so I could peer outside—into the farmyard, the stables, the Ruthenian church on the left and the sheds on the right. Seldom was the snow blanket injured, pierced by steps so early in the morning. Only the child, who was two, at most three years old, believed that the snow felt pain when a human being or a horse set foot in it. I realized that this was unavoidable, and I did it myself, certainly. But even today, I still look for a trodden path to avoid injuring the snow.

The purity of the snow, which the Pole in my novel talks about, had more than an ethical significance for the sensitive Jewish child in the East Galician shtetl. It wasn't just the beauty of the intact snow, un-touched by anyone or anything; nor was it the brightness radiating from the snow at night and on dark winter mornings. It was something else; it had something to do with the ubiquitous poverty, with the filth and ugliness of our shtetl. All these things vanished, became invisible—the shtetl was beautiful as soon as it was shrouded in snow. Its crooked roofs changed into hilly landscapes; its alleys and streets were covered with white carpets that concealed the holes and garbage heaps.

That was how I often spent the early morning hours, with the vast, immense world before me and close enough to touch the window-panes' frost flowers, which formed my concept of beauty earlier than anything else that my eyes had taken in. My father usually stood behind me, the prayer shawl over his shoulders and the black *tefillin* (small black leather box containing four passages from the Torah) on his forehead. The prayers he murmured were barely audible, but he ended each with a melody. I loved the Hasidic melodies. My father sang them as if even the saddest made him joyful, bringing peace to everything, like the warm radiance of unlimited kindness. In those days, I loved my father more than any living being, perhaps more than myself. And since then, I have never loved anyone as much as I loved him.

This morning, before it was even dawn, I was awakened by the sort of malaise caused by a dream of memory that leaves only a shadow. It was not hard to guess that my bad mood was linked to something I had written the day before yesterday. I found the manuscript, crept back into bed, and as soon as I opened the notebook I knew what was wrong. I felt troubled—as if I had committed an injustice that could have been easily avoided or instantly made up for.

The day before yesterday, when I mentioned its poverty, I also mentioned the filth and ugliness of the Jewish shtetl in which I spent the first ten years of my life. Zablotow was the name of this village, which was similar to hundreds of other tiny, crowded shtetls in which Jews lived until 1942 throughout Galicia, Russian Poland, Lithuania, White Russia and the Ukraine. Zablotow—its very name is unpleasant: it refers to the clayey soil, the unpaved streets, into which one could easily sink whenever they were softened by the endless autumn rains. Ninety percent of the three thousand inhabitants were Jews: artisans, more than might ever be needed, vendors rather than buyers—peddlers without capital, who normally hadn't yet paid for the goods they were hawking. They couldn't dispose of their wares because money grew scarcer and scarcer, because the Ruthenian farmers who came to the weekly market every Tuesday had too little to sell and could charge only low prices for their products. As a result, they couldn't buy more than salt herrings or a comb for a fiancée; once a year, a piece of clothing or a very cheap pair of shoes.

The inhabitants of Zablotow, like the Jews of any other shtetl, "lived on air," calling themselves *luftmenshn*, a Yiddish word that means "air people," those without any definite occupation. It would have been harder for them to do without their self-irony than their meager diet or shabby clothing.

Did I use the word *poverty* in connection with the shtetl? This term is misleading because it is so indequate. None of these people ever really ate their fill, although food was a lot cheaper there than in Western Europe. Many children dreamed of getting a brand-new piece of clothing, a brand-new pair of shoes once, just once in their lives. But it happened seldom if ever. Clothing was turned, then shortened, then turned again, repaired with suitable and often unsuitable patches—a vast harlequinade, which no one laughed at. The cheap tailors and cobblers were the busiest artisans; without them, many children would have had to go naked and without shoes, even in winter.

There were men who went without food not only on the countless fastdays, but also on every Monday and Thursday, partly so their children or grandchildren could have more to eat. When they baked the plaited challah for the Sabbath, they ate only as much of it as was necessary to justify the prescribed blessings; the rest was saved for the week, in case anyone fell ill. Children went barefoot until late autumn; in winter, one or two pairs of boots often had to make do for the entire family. Homes were heated with the cheapest brown coal and often the Jews couldn't even afford that. In every family, however, money did have to suffice for one thing: tuition. Starting at the age of three, boys (not girls) had to go to the *heder*, the Jewish elementary school, to learn how to read Hebrew, pray, and eventually translate the Bible.

We had all kinds of beggars: the "bashful" ones, who only wanted a loan, which they could never repay—not even the usually tiny sums that one could scarcely refuse them, not the flour and not the potatoes. Then there were the professional beggars, locals and itinerants, who usually appeared in groups, especially when well-to-do families married off a child or buried a relative. There were the poor who starved and froze silently. They lived on "miracles," which always came, though sometimes too late; a small remittance from a relative, an inheritance that brought them a few crowns, or the greatest, most hoped-for miracle: the children moved abroad and kept sending their needy parents tiny sums of money.

No matter how many people went hungry, no one starved to death. It was said that members of the community woke the rabbi early one morning lamenting: "Something terrible has happened. Someone has died of hunger right in our midst. His dead body was just found in his home."

The rabbi replied, "That can't be true. Why, it's impossible. Would you or you have refused to give him a piece of bread if he had asked for it?"

"No," they said, "but Eliezer was too proud to ask for anything."

"Well, then don't say that someone has died of hunger in our midst. Eliezer perished because of his pride."

Some people were indeed that proud, but they were few and far between. Most people just barely scraped by until they got help from their children, in America, or until they died of a lung disease or heart attack.

It was a grotesque, absurdly terrible *impoverishment*—but not poverty, because the Jews of Zablotow not only believed but *knew* that their condition was only temporary: soon everything would change, even though the misery had been going on for decades if not centuries—actually since the victory of the Cossack hetman Bogdan Chmielnicki in 1648. God, their God, of course, always intervened. Late, very late, but never *too* late. Beyond that, they could count on the arrival of the Messiah at any moment, hence on the ultimate salvation. In the countless prayer rooms and study rooms in every shtetl, there were always people who, during the endless conversations between afternoon and evening prayers, demonstrated that the excessive trouble and suffering confirmed the inevitable approach of the Messiah. Some of the people listening may have been skeptical and faint-hearted, worried they might die before the Redemption. But there was scarcely anyone who didn't believe in the Messiah and his imminent coming.

They stood in the candle-lit house of prayer; the soft singsong with which young men accompanied their study of the Talmud disturbed the zealous debaters as little as did the playing children, whose noise was tolerated even more readily because some of them had only recently lost a father or a mother. The orphan boys had to repeat the prayer for the dead three times a day, loudly, clearly. And if the text was too difficult for them, someone would help them along word for word. Singsong and children's noise and, not infrequently, a loud argument—none of this bothered the debaters, for they were absorbed in discussing everything, their own affairs and those of the wide world. Whether talking about themselves or the others, the "great ones," they always seasoned their plaintiveness with self-irony, their bombast with mockery. On Sundays, these men did not know how they would get their families through the new week, and on Thursdays, they racked their brains about finding the wherewithal to prepare for the Sabbath. These destitute men, who usually married too young and fathered children incessantly, were not poor in spirit, for they knew they would be part of the *olam haba,* the afterlife to which they would be admitted after dying. And if the Messiah arrived first, then the "next world" would open to them that much sooner.

When I think back to those Jews, whom I saw daily until the age of ten in the streets, the marketplace, the houses of prayer and study, then I recall two noises: sighs, lots of sighs and moans, but also laughter, kindly or derisive, yet always loud laughter, with sighs and moans soon joining in. Every bon mot (*git-vertl* in Yiddish) was instantly taken up, repeated, and relished, until it was finally replaced by a new one. Aside from the bon mots, these men often quoted wise, deep, and very astute statements. Hasidim brought them from the courts of their *tsadik*, the miracle-working rabbi, to whom they traveled again and again. Or else they quoted books and articles, mostly by Hebrew writers, or apocryphal utterances attributed to one "sharp mind" or another. The educated usually embellished their protracted speeches by quoting authors who didn't quite fit. They venerated Schiller, the sublime poet of ideals, more than anyone else. They also often cited Goethe, but not without some embarrassment because of his questionable love life. Heine, finally, was often mentioned, with pride, but mostly with painful scorn. He had converted to Christianity; he wasn't forgiven, it was never forgotten.

Whatever might happen over there in the wide world was eagerly discussed in every synagogue and in the marketplace. The shtetl Jews were interested in everything, even though they had little part in other people's events, wealth, or luxury. These Jews lived at the extreme edge of the world, they knew they did, but that didn't prevent them from taking vehement positions and imagining, at least during the endless debates, that their opinions mattered too. These "air people" lived in the realm of an "as if" that metamorphosed everything.

As I have said, talking about the ugliness of the shtetl has troubled me, even in my sleep. What did the Jews themselves think of the shtetl? Did they know how ugly their houses were, how unsightly their poor clothes? Naturally, they lacked any possibility of comparison for most of them never traveled more than twenty miles away, perhaps once or twice, before they died. They didn't like the surrounding countryside; in their eyes, the thatched huts of the Ukrainians were a lot uglier than their own houses. Moreover, they avoided those villages as much as possible, because they rightfully feared hostility. Nevertheless, the shtetls were not ghettoes; indeed, they were the very opposite, both in essence and by definition. A shtetl was not an appendage within lawful precincts to a Christian community, it was not an alien body, discriminated against within a higher culture. On the contrary, it was a clearly defined autonomous community with its own culture—amid poverty and ugliness and surrounded by enemies of the Jewish faith. The shtetl was a center, and the Jews saw the Slavic villages as peripheral agglomerates whose inhabitants, mostly illiterate, had no relationship to the world of the intellect.

In all its misery, the shtetl was a tiny civitas dei, amazing in mind and spirit, centuries behind the times in certain respects, sometimes re-pulsive, and yet admirable, because the lives of these people were ruled by their truly exemplary devotion to a relentlessly demanding faith, daily, nay, hourly, down to the slightest detail. The Jews in the ghettoes of Venice, or Rome, or Worms remained a minority in their home cities, exiled and discriminated against. But the Jews in a shtetl formed a majority, they were at home. Their gentile neighbors, the Polish aristo-crats, for instance, might be powerful and wealthy and look down on them. But the Jews were convinced of their own superiority. They had no sense of inferiority whatsoever about being Jews, and thus they didn't have the slightest desire to conceal who and what they were or to become like the others.

Normally, two families lived together, sometimes in a single room. The arguments of the women, who had to cook on the same stove, the screams of the children—all this noise could be heard out in the street, day and night. Unhappiness was always made public; happiness often remained private, but it was urged on everyone else whenever parents could boast about their offspring. Children were scolded loudly; they were even cursed and, almost in the same breath, showered with the most affectionate words.

Most of the houses had only one story and seldom more than two small rooms and a kitchen; they were made of wood and the roofs were shingled. These homes were crowded together, as if each were seeking protection with the others. The streets seldom ran in straight lines, for every house looked as if it were trying to be different, at least in its shape. It all seemed right out of a town planner's nightmare.

There was no gas, no electricity, no sewer in the shtetl, and naturally no indoor plumbing. There were just a few wells, where the Jews obtained their water. Carriers delivered it to those families that could afford them, and the Jews kept it in large barrels inside their homes. The poor had to get water themselves.

These wooden houses were fire traps—in any season, but especially in winter when the defective stoves caused fires. Since the wells were far away, and the water often froze in the barrels, the blaze couldn't be doused in time. The winds carried it from home to home, and for an entire night, the shtetl might be surrounded by flames leaping into the sky. Reddish yellow walls kept rising higher, sinking down into the darkness, and then climbing up again. In their light, one could see half-naked men, who were sometimes concentrated in a dense cluster, as though they mustn't separate, and yet they soon scurried apart—to the wells, to the burning houses, or to people who were unscathed but threatened. The night turned into day, the children couldn't sleep either; they ran through the streets, gathering near the blazes or dragging the empty buckets to the wells.

During such nights, I learned that if terrible misfortune remains an isolated event rather than turning into a condition, the victims become so agitated that they act as if the orderly world were out of joint because it has lost all its laws.

I had been told that whenever great fires break out, angels settle on the roof, ridge, and gable of the *Hoikhe Shul* in order to protect the only synagogue in the shtetl. God's messengers then assume the guise of white doves.

I must have been four years old the first time that, like so many other children, I slipped out of the house unhindered and ran through the streets to the large well, where water was being pumped for hoses and pails, and out to the streets that shone red in the fire.

I was drawn mainly to the synagogue, to the guardian angels. Naturally, I didn't doubt they existed, but I wanted to see them myself and watch them saving the house of God. At last, I stood at the foot of the hill on which the synagogue had been erected long, long ago. We almost never prayed there, but I often went in alone to admire the frescoes—they were the first paintings I had ever seen.

I could hear the disquieting creaks of the burning rafters, the façade of the synagogue was brightly lit, the reflections of flames leaped up and down in the high windows. But all this was unimportant to the child who stared excitedly at the white doves protecting the synagogue. They were as white as morning's pure snow. Even adults seemed to believe that these birds were angels who came flying down from heaven whenever there was a fire. For the children staring up at the doves and observing each of their movements, this was as certain as their own existence.

I am not quite sure that I shared their faith, although everything I did or didn't do was no less ruled by religious shalts and shalt-nots, so that I could scarcely imagine being a Jew and not living as we did. And yet, during one of those burning nights, I felt the glimmer of doubt. Granted, everything was as it should be. The doves remained on the roof and over the large portal. The synagogue didn't burn, even though the wind drove the fire along. And that, Jews said, was how the angels had been guarding it against all dangers for centuries.

Conjecturing about the cause of my doubt would be useless, for I can scarcely verify anything. I myself owned a pair of white doves, a present from my father when we had moved into our new home—and I knew that doves could not be angels. But in that red night, which was hung with black streamers, I experienced the sensation of faith and the gratification of witnessing a miracle. A short while later, however, perhaps just a few minutes, everything changed; I was only witnessing the fact that the *others* believed in the miracle. How early did I catch myself in the contradiction of passionate affirmation and dispassionate skepticism? I couldn't say.

Heder—the word means *room*. It refers to the Jewish elementary school, usually run by a destitute man, an "air person," in a single room, where his wife and countless children lived, ate, and slept. The pupils were at least three years old and seldom more than six. Later, they studied under a qualified teacher in some heder that was more like a classroom, but seldom like a class. I didn't want to go to heder, partly, no doubt, because I was very spoiled at home, but chiefly because of the endless poverty and depressing ugliness. For the first time, I learned that most children did not eat their fill, that they suffered from skin ailments that disfigured their faces. I experienced revulsion at an early age and discovered that it was accompanied by fear, by an anxiety, that was hard to grasp. In order to get me to the heder without actually forcing me, they hit on the idea of having the teacher's factotum, the so-called *belfer* (assistant), carry me there on his back. A belfer was usually a young man who was incapable of doing anything and could expect nothing out of life. Once he told me that I should treat him like a horse. He capered about, galloped, whinnying rather woefully. Since he was my mount, I had to feed him, of course. I was glad to feed him because I usually had no appetite, and I was delighted to empty my pouch, making it look as if I had eaten my lunch. But I also enjoyed letting my "horse" think that his playacting had enticed me into giving him my food.

The three-year-old never let on that he only pretended to go along with the joke. A few years later, I gave up "riding," and preferred to walk to heder, for I now needed my lunch for Berele. He was "big," maybe six years old, a starving little fox. He soon discovered me; naturally, he knew that my parents were well off. He became my protector, never deserting me. The same game was repeated every day: He was the dancing bear that I led on a chain through towns and villages. He obeyed only me, in exchange for which I had to give him my lunch—I even had to stuff it into his mouth. Berele, whose small eyes were always peering about for something, was one of many children of an *agunah*, a deserted wife. If no trace of her husband was found, she would have to remain single the rest of her life.

I loved Berele very much: I loved his lightning-fast movements, his pranks, his skill in mimicking adults. He was probably the first con man I ever met. He wheedled toys out of me, then sold them; he got my allowance, always promising to give me the most wonderful things in exchange—for instance, a real rifle. I was generally considered a very bright child, but for the little con man I was an easy target. Actually, I soon saw through him but didn't disillusion him. And even later, I never let on that I had found him out soon enough. Why didn't I? I must have felt the superiority as well as the great enjoyment we derive from a secret superiority.

That summer we went to a health resort as usual, and that autumn I was no longer sent to the heder, where Berele carried out his complicated plots. I must have bumped into him now and then, but the friendship was over. He seemed to be avoiding me, I didn't know why, and I soon made friends with other children, mostly from well-to-do families, whose parents were friendly with mine. But I have never forgotten Berele, not only because he was the one who paved my way to psychology, but also because of the Messianic gymnastics he practiced with me. Like the adults, we children knew that the Messiah might descend to earth at any moment. Our salvation would begin with the "reversal of the world." Berele concluded that we would all suddenly walk upside down. In order to prepare for this unpleasant situation, we should practice standing on our heads ahead of time, Berele explained; that way, we would get into the correct position when the big moment came. Under his guidance, I learned how to walk on my hands until I got dizzy.

I left the faith at an early age, thirteen, joining the revolutionary movement and taking on a great deal in my political devotion. But I often thought of Berele's upside-down exercises. I had long since given up obeying the countless laws that govern the everyday life of pious Jews. But my faith in the Messiah was still as powerful as ever. Our Messianic

equivalent was revolutionary activity. In everything I now learned, experienced, and undertook, I never stopped seeking reasons for Messianic
faith. Perhaps I still do so today. Perhaps, since I first began thinking, I
have never encountered any idea that so utterly overwhelmed me and so
persistently governed my direction as the idea that this world cannot
remain as it is, and that it *can* become different, better, and that it *will*
become different and better.

I mentioned the episode of the doves on the endangered synagogue
only to emphasize that I was seized with doubt in a moment of a
seemingly visible miracle. Actually, however, that dramatic situation
could not fully explain why my faith was increasingly undermined even
though doubt did not become especially visible or even disturbing to the
child whose harmonious life felt safe and sound. This is so true that only
now, when thinking and writing about the remote past, am I fully aware
that I was a "sinner" in my childhood and a skeptic to boot, yet with no
bad conscience toward other people or God, in whom I believed as
naturally as in the sky overhead.

Sinner, I said. A memory surfaces; it was probably never fully
buried, just temporarily absent. I recalled it several years ago when I tried
to accurately gauge the role of sexuality in my youth and in later years and
to understand what was peculiar about it.

The experience I now recall occurred at about the same time—that
is, between the ages of three and four—as the other episodes I have
mentioned. And I can determine with a high degree of probability the
age at which this far-reaching if seemingly unimportant incident took
place. It was a Day of Atonement, it must have been Yom Kippur 1909.
For some reason—I may have been sick or convalescing—I had not been
taken along to the house of prayer. It was an unusually hot autumn day.
Hanusia, the Ukrainian maid, was out in the garden with me, behind the
house. She lay half propped up under an apple tree. I sat next to her. I
don't know how the strange game began, but it was probably she who
pulled me over and pushed my hand under her dress, on her naked breast.
She must have then changed her position, so that my hands glided over
her belly and her thighs. I felt a pleasure that I was not to experience
again until much later—an excitement as if my whole body were on fire.
Everything melted, the heat of the scorching sun rays, the warmth of the
smooth, soft skin of that large, clumsy girl, and the unknown delight that
permeated my limbs, my entire body, confusing me, sweeping me away—
I didn't know why or where.

When Hanusia then shook me off, I discovered red spots in her face and something unusual in her eyes: she squinted as she peered all around, terrified. Silently we went indoors. Soon the worshipers came back to rest during the long recess between morning prayers and the prayers that follow for many long hours until nightfall.

I realized that I had certainly done something that was forbidden, and also that Hanusia would keep the incident to herself. So I never told anyone about it—not then, not later; not ever.

I knew that this sin was even greater becaue I had committed it on a day of penitence and expiation, on Yom Kippur, a day of awe. Yet I didn't really have a guilty conscience. Naturally, I believed in an all-knowing, punishing God as steadfastly as I believed that rain was wet and ice was cold. But I did not fear God, not him or his punishments. Somewhat later, and it happened more than once, I climbed up to the barn roof and hurled stones at the sky with all my might, hoping a stone would hit him: God would be annoyed, open a trapdoor, and glare down at me. I was determined to stand up to him, even reproach him, for holding back the Messiah, without whom we couldn't endure much longer. I never told anyone about my challenge to God.

My relationship to Hanusia remained what it had been previously, as if nothing had happened under the apple tree. I may have secretly been grateful to her, but I don't remember. Nothing changed for me after that first sexual experience, although it must have been crucial, because tactility assumed unusual importance in all my erotic and sexual attachments.

Not the only crucial experience, but *one* crucial experience. It was probably because of the extremely unhealthy living conditions that so many shtetl children suffered from skin diseases. As far back as I can remember, the sight of unhealthy skin has always aroused my violent disgust and fear of contact. I had certainly been warned at an early age of the effects of dirt and therefore of too close a contact with the children of poor people. But this does not fully explain why I hid a skin abrasion (say, on an injured finger) from myself, why I found a tiny, barely visible brown dot on the back of my hand so unbearable that I tried to cut it out with a knife. As I write this, I glance at my hands, which are covered with large and small brown spots—the hands of an elderly man. Have I become reconciled with them? Perhaps I am indifferent to them now—through that process of detachment which has estranged me from my face and, more and more, from my body.

Even before my experience in the garden, I had always been drawn to smooth, white skin, but felt an extremely intense repugnance when anything struck me as ugly. A wart on a face, a crooked mouth, a boil— all these things made me uneasy. I looked away from such faces in- stinctively, as I do today when I am angry with someone or know that he is lying to me.

I still can't look at clowns. The sight of them caused one of the first truly shattering disappointments of my early childhood. At last, a circus had come to the shtetl. No day had ever seemed so long to me as the day on which my father would be taking us to the circus in the evening. We would see wild animals and wild people, dwarfs, horses dancing waltzes or polkas as they carried women dressed like princesses; jugglers and trapeze artists and a man who played ten instruments at once—and last, but far from least: the clowns. And here they were! Their costumes were even more ragged and more gaudily patched than the clothes of our poorest beggars; their faces were deformed by thick paint, and they had red potatoes instead of noses. Their pranks were certainly very funny, the most comical one being the resurrection of the dead clown who carried candles in his own funeral procession and, with the others, loudly bewailed his own death. All this was wonderful. But even today I still find it as difficult to see a clown's arbitrarily distorted face as to look into the eyes of a person who feels humiliated. Fear and anxiety are certainly part of my reaction.

But, as I have said, I felt neither fear nor anxiety after that strange event on the Day of Atonement. I believed in God's omnipotence and yet I did not hesitate to defy him, for instance by touching a candelabra on a Friday evening or (secretly, of course) scribbling something with a pencil on paper or on a piece of furniture. In all these ways, I was, I knew, desecrating the Sabbath and committing a sin.

Was I merely flirting with danger? That could be, for even infants enjoy this game: evoking terror and cheerfully delighting in overcoming it. Nevertheless, I was certain that the almighty creator of the world belonged to us—he was a Jewish god, committed to my ancestors since time immemorial and hence to their descendants. I feared God, to be sure, but in the same way that I feared my father, needing to be liked by him, never disliked. Nevertheless, I kept doing things that my father prohibited. I was bad, but I never had to fear that he would stay angry with me for long; I had realized soon enough that he felt punished when he had to punish me. The confidence he inspired in me was boundless; it has determined all my relationships with people throughout my life.

When I looked away from the frost flowers and the snowy world on those winter mornings he shared with me, I did so to look at him. His head was always covered with a *yarmulke,* a dark blue velvet skullcap, or a black silk toque; his face was framed by a fashionably trimmed black beard. Although he was rigorously observant because of his Hasidic background, he never had earlocks, nor did he ever wear a gaberdine, except on the Sabbath and on holidays. He dressed in what was known as the "European" manner. His light brown eyes behind the gold-edged pince-nez always seemed to smile when he looked at you, a smile that was often ironic, but usually kind. From the very start, his eyes inspired courage in the hypersensitive child, courage and the desire to be cheerful and bright. I carried his trust like a burden, a very precious load. I always told myself that he thought too highly of me, and I did everything possible not to disappoint him. I could hurt anyone, but not him.

Every Friday afternoon, all the men went to the steam bath to prepare for the Sabbath by thoroughly cleaning away the dirt of weekdays. When you entered it, you collided with a terrible din; a wall of almost opaque steam blurred the outlines, the heat took the child's breath away. The wooden benches rose in tiers; the higher the bench, the hotter the air. The children usually remained on the lower benches. My father boasted to his friends that I was tough enough to climb up to the highest level and even stay there for several minutes. Ah, I wasn't tough, but how could I disappoint him? I didn't fear his reproaches, but I so ardently wanted to find the good, warm smile of approval in his eyes. While I was still very young, he always expected me, encouraged me, to say something unusual—something very bright about people and things, to be quick-witted in answering, but not fresh or precocious.

Our home, it seems today, was always full of people—especially in the evening. I often felt my father's eyes gazing at me expectantly. I kept wanting to tell him that he should expect nothing of me, that I was far from being as smart as he thought. Until I was twelve, these words were always on the tip of my tongue, and yet—though it may seem unlikely, it is true—I never uttered them. As a child, I never had the courage to disappoint his expectations. Did he know, did he ever suspect how hard he made things for me? He died at seventy-eight, but I never asked him. Indeed, we never spoke even one syllable about the relationship that tied us so closely together until it was finally shattered because of me.

Furthermore, at five and six years of age, I was expected to sing beautifully and articulate the words precisely. That was easier than anything else. For along with the completely rigorous observance of all ritual, religious, and traditional shalts and shalt-nots, our home, no less than the poorest in the shtetl, was always filled with singing, in almost every situation, from morning to evening. The singing emerged from all the places of prayer and study, from the basements of the poorest workers, from the back courts and stables. The religious melodies the exiles had brought from the Orient blended uniquely with the songs sung by the Slavic host nations, especially the Ukrainian peasants.

"When does a Jew sing?" one would ask, and the answer was: "He sings when he's hungry." Interestingly enough, the word *Jew* was sometimes replaced by the word *peasant*. By which we really only meant the Ukrainian peasant. Sometimes the answer was: "He sings when (or because) he is sad."

There were new Jewish folk songs all the time, and they remained faithful to the people who wanted not only to bemoan its unspeakably difficult struggle for day-to-day survival, but also to sing about it: the arduous effort to earn food for the family and tuition for the children; the woe and weal of being a Jew in a hostile world; the pain of leaving one's place of birth to escape poverty; and finally, homesickness for Palestine or yearning for the free land of America, where "they eat white bread even on weekdays." Both America and *di alte heym* [the old country] produced the revolutionary songs: they wandered from the wretched places of work into the street, spreading like wildfire:

> *Du shpinst ois die vol*
> *un host dokh keyn kleyd,*
> *du bakst dos broit*
> *dokh hungern tustu.*

> You spin the wool
> yet you don't have clothes,
> you bake the bread
> yet you starve to death.

And that was where the lovesongs came from with their coy sensuality, their promise of happiness, their grief over forced divorce, over unfaithfulness, desertion. Jews sang about everything, and their songs were both ironic and grandiloquent, defiant and woeful. Singing was a part of life, which was reflected in songs; we sought refuge, new courage, in them. Some of the lyrics were by famous Yiddish and Hebrew poets, but most had been created by the people—the resigned and the rebellious, the happy and unhappy lovers.

The first songs I heard and effortlessly warbled without the words were Hebrew and Aramaic chants that were part of the liturgy. At some point every evening, one of the guests might interrupt an overly vehement argument or a game of cards by breaking into a song, with the others then joining in. A second and third song might follow, and they sometimes continued until late at night or—in the summer—until early morning. However, on every Friday evening we entertained not only my father's friends, but also my grandfather's old companions. They drank beer or mead, sometimes also a very strong brandy. The white candles in the high-stemmed silver holders slowly burned out. Sometimes, the company remained in the dark, discussing the political events, working themselves up for or against Zionism, which made tempers flare. They had intricate debates about various interpretations of a biblical or Talmudic line, citing innumerable commentators. But eventually they would launch into song again. It was both prayer, comfort, and lament.

> And do you know, Dreyfus,
> Why this is happening to you?
> Only because you're
> Only because you're a Jew.

We children were allowed to stay up until we fell asleep, and we were then put to bed.

On some Friday evenings, my father's grandfather would show up, always unannounced. He was already over eighty when I knew him. A long, white beard covered his chest. When he threw his head back while talking, you could see a dark or snow-white silk string on his collar. His eyes were youthful—and terrifying whenever he grew angry or simply disagreed with some opinion. Otherwise, however, his eyes were attentive—they even had a childlike curiosity. Once, as a rabbi, he had had a falling-out with his congregation because it had tolerated an opponent of the Hasidic rebbe whose follower and friend he was. That same night, my outraged great-grandfather had left the town, reaching his birthplace after a long, dangerous ride through the Carpathian mountains. He rejected any attempt at reconciliation until the end of his life. When one of his sons took over that same rabbinate, the old man chose to ignore this altogether. He spent his life "learning," that is, studying the holy books and their commentaries, which was one reason he retired from the world. Every day, at the crack of dawn, he would dash out of his house to take a quick, cold plunge. He dashed because he had no time. When a doctor told the old man to curb his eagerness, he declared, "I haven't got a minute to lose, for now I'm finally beginning to *really* understand. Now the essence is finally being revealed to me."

Yes, Reb Borekh ran, not just because he didn't have a minute to spare from his studies, but also because he wanted to avoid other people. He couldn't stand banality and triviality. He seldom went to the house of prayer; he did his praying in his study. Sometimes as evening came on, he might go out, wearing his white smock, and hurry to the hill to see if the Messiah was coming. The Messiah didn't have to come precisely at that time of day, but there was no moment in which he might not come. I don't know whether my great-grandfather felt disappointed as he headed home.

This old man, the only compelling authority I have ever encountered—not only in my childhood but in my entire life—was the hero of many stories that I loved to hear. All these tales emphasized that he was wise and learned and completely indifferent to everything other people set store by: honors, money, social standing. Yet he was unwilling, if not unable, to accept any compromise when it came to faith, doctrine, and devotion. He never hid his impatience when he had to listen to stupid or uneducated people, especially if they were well-to-do and pretentious. On the other hand, he always listened carefully to the words of the poor and unfortunate who sought his advice and comfort. When he encountered a suffering human being, his arrogance, usually so palpable, yielded to an uncharacteristic respect.

When I think back to this medium-sized man in the black gaberdine with the heavy silk belt, think back to the amazing agility of his movements, the speed with which he shook off other people, then I feel certain that, in the midst of the shtetl, where people lived so crowded together that they could scarcely avoid one another for even a single day, he must have been lonelier than anyone I have ever met.

What had brought such isolation upon that old man? Not the assault by enemies, much less any fear of them, because he was certain of his cause and its imminent victory. It must have been his inability to overcome the gap separating him from people with whom he would have liked to be friends. He never forgave them for not living up to the demands whose fulfillment he saw as the sole justification of life. He was wrong, I am sure of that now. But if I had remained in the shtetl, and if it had not changed, who knows whether I might not think as he did. I tell myself that I have often been no less severe than he was, though I had a lot less reason and right.

In a certain sense, my great-grandfather was responsible for the beginning of my "career," whatever this may have been. For one spring day, when the lilac was glowing through a side window of his study, he declared that I would be an *ilui,* a luminary of Israel. I must have been six and a half at the time. Every Sunday, like all Jewish boys my age, I was starting to translate a more or less sizable chunk of the weekly Torah portion that would be read aloud on the following Sabbath by the prayer leader in the house of prayer. The children were expected to learn their lesson by Friday. One Tuesday my teacher discovered that I already knew the text and its translation by heart. He was so impressed that he risked bringing me to my great-grandfather unannounced, so that he could "test me" (the Yiddish word for this is *farhern*).

The six decades separating me from that hour have scarcely wiped a single detail from my memory. I can see myself standing in front of the heavy table with the old tomes; next to me stood the teacher, an extremely tall man, who would glance expectantly at me and then try to catch my great-grandfather's eye. Naturally, I wanted to please them; but more important, more unsettling was again having to do something in order not to disappoint someone else's expectations. I succeeded. I was allowed to step behind the table, my great-grandfather placed his right hand on my head, his lips moved—probably murmuring a blessing. Then he paid the teacher a richly allusive compliment, adding his prophecy as he pointed at me. The teacher took me straight to my father's office, and I again had to reel off the text and the translation.

Word of Rabbi Borekh's praise had already gotten around the shtetl.

As a result, I was more frightened than ever that my father and now my great-grandfather would think too highly of me and sooner or later realize their mistake. I often wished that this would happen very soon, immediately, to relieve me of my burden and fear.

The memory of my grandfather's eyes is still compelling. He looked at me coolly, then with moderate amazement. But all at once, something lit up in his eyes, making me blissful. I have never forgotten this feeling.

His prophecy did not come true—I did not become an *ilui.* As I have said, in my early adolescence, I broke with the faith that meant everything to him, and I have never sought another faith. Thus I realized early enough that I was not "designated," although there have always been people who thought I was. That is why I believed, and still do, that I may share some bad qualities with my great-grandfather, but not his resistance to every temptation, not the courage to close myself off hermetically from all trivia, and not the strange modesty that was so naturally tied to his arrogance.

Even as a child, I had no desire ever to become like him. But looking back on my accomplishments, I set great store in telling myself that while he might not have agreed with me, he certainly would not have despised what I have achieved in my best moments. Perhaps it was not only vanity that temporarily made me assume, made me hope that I deserved that look—certainly not always, but sometimes.

In contrast to him, I have always needed to live in harmony with my friends. It makes me suffer to disagree with them about essential things. Yet I certainly owe my great-grandfather the decisive strength and will power not to waver in a conviction, even if no one wants to share it with me. He must have borne loneliness far more easily than his great-grandson could, perhaps because he was actually never alone: he felt God's presence as distinctly as the hand he kept placing on his eyes that were weary from "learning." This educated, perspicacious, and unusually intelligent man could imagine anything except sincere godlessness, that is, living and thinking as if the creator of the world did not exist.

Every year before Passover, we "learned," read, and translated the Song of Songs. For children there was nothing improper about this passionate love song, for, thanks to the oral tradition accompanying the singsong translation, they discovered what the text was really about: not the love between a man and a woman, of course, but the falling-out between God and His chosen people, which has sinned, and is wandering through the nocturnal streets, like the woman in the Song of Songs, seeking her beloved, that is, God. She stops every passerby to ask where her beloved is, and she eventually reaches the closed gates of the town. But the watchmen mock her and her beloved, whom no one has ever seen.

My great-grandfather too could sometimes strive against his God, as the Rebbe of Berdychev had dared to do in his Yiddish prayers. Had my great-grandfather learned that I hurled stones at heaven to call God out and gaze into his angry face, he probably wouldn't have considered this blasphemy. The Almighty was everywhere; even a child would have to bump into him, perhaps even offend and come to blows with him. I was virtually taking dictation from Rabbi Borekh when I wrote the dying words of Rabbi Binye, an adolescent hero of my novel, to his comrade-in-arms, a nonreligious Viennese Jew: "Poor man, you're all alone now. How are you going to live without God?"

Of course, whatever the Jews in the shtetl were like, in many ways they resembled the Gentiles of the community. They differed from them mainly by being "permanent worshipers." The men devoted the first hour of the day and another, before and after the onset of evening, to prayer. In between there were countless opportunities for benedictions: when washing hands before a meal; prior to placing the first piece of bread in your mouth; drinking the first drop; eating the first fresh fruit of the year—there was no end of blessings. Most texts were in Hebrew, a few in Aramaic. *Kaddish*, the prayer for the dead, spoken by the male offspring for one year after the death of a close relative, was what impressed me the most. Orphan boys, even those who had only just begun to talk, were brought to the house of prayer every morning and evening to recite the Kaddish for a dead person, a prematurely deceased father or mother. Even as I write these lines, I am overcome by the deep emotion I felt when listening to the orphans stammering and stuttering their way through this long prayer in front of the mute worshipers.

However, since I understood the text at a very early age, it always made me ill at ease whenever I heard it, and eventually I felt the same about nearly all prayers. A human being had died, innocent, snatched away by an incurable disease; the survivors remained penniless, at the mercy of boundless destitution. And now, three times a day, they had to repeat Kaddish, which begins with the words, "Exalted and sanctified be the name of the Creator . . . ," and goes on with the flattery and adulation that abound in most prayers of all religions.

Around the time my great-grandfather discovered me, so to speak, I felt my first doubts. Why did God need to have stammering, wretched orphans keep incessantly repeating that He alone was great, was wonderful, that He alone had created the universe, that His will alone ruled; that He alone had led the Jews to freedom from Egypt and given them the land of Canaan for their own, and so forth. All too often I heard the flattery with which poor people approached my father, and, whether the sycophants hoped to derive some advantage immediately or later on, I found them repulsive. They believed they were exalting the person before whom they were humbling themselves. And God supposedly wished for the same thing, indeed demanded it—morning, afternoon, dusk, and even at night, and even from children who had to praise him though they couldn't keep their eyes open?

Yet there was the liturgical solemnity, its mood ruling everything by way of the chant. Because of this solemnity—not the words—I enjoyed and was often deeply moved by the cantors. It made no difference how clearly they articulated the text, it did not concern me—I no longer heeded the words. There *were* exceptions, for instance the *piyus*, that is, medieval poems, and the psalms, which were included, especially on holidays. I loved many of the psalms and, in fact, I have never stopped singing them. (If I manage to carry out my long-term plans, I intend to translate a selection of psalms into French and German.)

I remember the spring of 1933 in Berlin—I have seldom known a lovelier spring. Like many other people, I was in prison. There were no concentration camps as yet. Each of us assumed that at some point, probably early one morning, he would be taken out of solitary con-finement and be shot "while trying to escape." Then it happened. The day was waning, SS men together with a large number of guards had gathered under the swastika flag for the evening roll call in the prison yard. And now the *Horst Wessel Song*, sung by that chorus, penetrated my cell, clearly and ominously. I had heard it many times, of course, but at that moment it seemed like a prayer—that is, I ignored the words and listened only to the old and now misused military tune. When darkness fell, and the light went out in my cell, a psalm urged itself to my lips, as if coming from outside myself:

> Where is your God,
> Our God is in heaven
> As well as on earth,
> He does His will.

First, I listened to myself in ironic amazement, but then I let myself go. That night I went through all the psalms I knew by heart, singing them softly to myself, and then recited the night prayer in which, during my childhood, I had listed the archangels who were to watch over me and my sleep, at the head and foot of my bed. In the hypnagogic slumber from which I would eventually pass into a profound sleep, I heard the songs; they broke into one another or blended strangely. The lullaby promising the baby that his father "will send a letter from America with twenty dollars and his portrait" merged with the vulgar hit of that spring: "When the village band plays on Sunday evening. . . ." But upon awakening, I again recalled the songs of my childhood. They haunted me, filling many hours of my imprisonment. I sang all their stanzas until I was too tired to continue, and I went back to them as soon as I had recovered my strength. No, they did not arouse my nostalgia for the distant past or the shtetl that I had left seventeen years earlier. I will obviously never see it again, but it remains in my memory, in series and mixtures of colors and images and tones, and I am still amazed at their variety.

There were domestic animals in the shtetl: geese and chickens, goats, cows, and horses. Compared with the human beings, they all struck me as ugly and silly, except for the horses. I saw the horses as the most perfect creatures on earth; I am not certain that I have changed my mind: "Doino often thought back to a string of wounded horses being led through the small town after a battle, he thought of a mare whose eyes had run out. He had wept for this animal, the way the dead would weep for themselves if they consciously experienced their deaths."

And today, like this hero of my novel, I am still deeply upset when I think of wounded or starving horses. "It's hard to be a Jew." This Yiddish proverb was often repeated, with a sigh. Sometimes you added, "It's hard to be a Jewish horse," that is, a horse belonging to an "air person," who, as the joke went, had to make sure his poor draft animal never learned that there was such a thing as oats, an unaffordable luxury.

One summer, I frequently led a buckskin down to the shore of the Prut to water it. His shaggy hair was always clean and shiny. He liked being mounted by children and he patiently put up with their abrupt gestures. He was kind, good-natured, and understanding. You could tell by his big, attentive eyes.

I think I knew at a very early age that children were conceived by a sexual act. Wherever you looked, you could see roosters jumping hens; you often saw the ludicrous spectacle of a pair of dogs that seemed unable to pry themselves apart. Yet I was always stunned if not confused by the sight of horses copulating in the barnyard, near the stable. Strange, if not bewildering, was the fact that both animals trembled as if the stallion were as frightened as the mare. When it finally succeeded and was over, the adults congratulated one another; the owner of the stallion received the compliments as if he himself had pulled off some marvelous feat.

During that same period I, like so many other children, often witnessed the dramatic event of a colt or calf being wrested from the body of a mare or cow. I was so deeply moved by the sufferings of these animal mothers that even today I associate unbearable physical pain with help-lessly suffering animals. I don't mean to give the wrong impression: I am not what you would call an animal lover. In my eyes, only man is an incomparable living creature—the most valuable on this earth.

Mayim khayim: that's what the "living water" that gushes from a wellspring was called by the Hebrew teacher they had hired from Vienna. The children could have their first outing under his supervision. It must have been around Pentecost. When I, the youngest pupil, looked at the gently sloping meadows, which became pastureland on the hills, the foothills of the Carpathian mountains, I first discovered how many different colors had the same name: green. Yet I was told these were only different shades. I had another lesson that same summery day in spring. When we climbed the hills, I glimpsed their highest peak, which seemed to touch the sky. The child who had so often secretly hurled stones at heaven without hitting it, was seized by an ineffable, shattering hope: once he arrived at the peak, he would reach the end of the world and thus the entrance to heaven. What happened then is something that count-less people have experienced before and after: the discovery that the sky remains equally high and remote from both the valley and the moun-tains, and that beyond these mountains there are more mountains, higher ones, the highest, concealing further mountains in turn—and so it goes, all over the world, endlessly. This very intense experience was not only a disappointment for the child, but also left him uneasy and in suspension.

"*Mayim Khayim,*" the teacher explained, "is the same clear water that has been gushing out here since time immemorial, and yet it is not and never will be the same water."

Just a few years later, in Vienna, forever removed from that well-spring, I was to learn something similar in my Greek class, and the two Hebrew words were replaced with Hellenic words: *panta rhei.* But earlier, among the Carpathian foothills, I began to sense, in my childish way of imagining things, that although one can experience truth, it changes as soon as you learn it, leaving only a hint, a signpost pointing to another truth concealed behind it—hill beyond hill, beyond hills, and none of them the final hill.

Our shtetl lay on the Prut, a tributary of the Danube. An iron bridge led the townsfolk to the opposite bank and the densely forested hills beyond. Sometimes, not often, we could spot loaded rafts floating down the Prut. My father promised me that some day I could ride a raft—for one day and one night. His promise never came true. One of the experiences that I, probably like every other human being, so ardently yearned for was a ride on a raft. Naturally, I could have gotten my wish later on, during adolescence or adulthood. But it is probably one of those wishes that you would rather nurture than realize.

People bathed on only one side of the river, our shore, not on the opposite one. The men, naked, to the right of the bridge; the women, in their long shirts, to the left. In the summer, when the days were mercilessly hot, the teacher sent the children to the river, but told them to plunge in only once or twice, and then instantly return to the heder. To save time, they pulled off their clothes on the spot, arriving naked in the marketplace. But it was no use—they had to get back before they were refreshed, for nothing was as important as "learning." And you don't let the Torah wait.

As long as I lived in the shtetl, it seemed the most natural thing in the world to see men naked in the steambath every Friday and at the river every summer day. No matter what their age, they moved uninhibitedly, in the most natural way. Very young children learned where babies come from. They were no more surprised than the children in the countryside. Many of them slept in the same room as their parents, some in the same bed. The poverty that forced this openness on them brought the children premature experiences, which they freely described to their affluent friends. As did, of course, my friend Berele, who thereby helped me to do sums in my head. He taught me that a man must sleep with his wife six times in order to have a boy and four times for a girl. I then had to figure out how often this man or that had had to *tren* [colloquial Yiddish for "screw"] the mother of his children, whose number and sexes we knew. The calculations interested Berele, and, under his influence, me too for several days—the calculations and the spirited way we used the vulgar word *"trenen."*

There was nothing shameful about sex; it was part of family life—and these children of strictly monogamous parents could not imagine human existence without a family. Parental sex may have frequently disturbed the sleep of the children, but their parents' arguments had a more lasting impact—the immense and violent arguments between husband and wife, whose poverty dramatized their laments, and, when all anger is dissipated, solace, reconciliation, and new courage are found in an embrace. The children suffered from these sometimes paroxysmal conflicts and did everything they could to avoid having to witness them. Yet they knew how loyal the opponents were to each other. During the day, an argument between his parents might have deafened and saddened a child; but when he was suddenly awakened at night, he told himself that now everything was fine again and the coming day would be peaceful. At a very early age, the poor children of the shtetl (and nearly all of them were poor) gained insights and experiences that helped them understand many things better than many well-to-do children who were later to become psychoanalysts. . . .

The iron bridge was the pride of the shtetl, yet everyone knew what would happen soon after the coming of the Messiah. There would suddenly be a second bridge, not iron, not stone, not even wood. No, it would be made of paper, yes indeed, cigarette paper. And the skeptics, the sinners, the blasphemers would naturally laugh at the paper bridge and choose the iron one. Yes, that was what they would do, and they would plunge into the water with the iron bridge and drown. But the pious, the people of faith, would not hesitate or be afraid, they would sing as they crossed the paper bridge into the happiness of everlasting life.

I knew exactly how thin my grandfather's cigarette paper was and how easily it tore. It came from France; its name was Riz-Abadie, and the package sported a soldier in wide red trousers. Now I was convinced that I was no blasphemer, no evildoer in Israel. So I had to believe that the paper bridge was the safe one. But, without telling my father's father, I decided I would cross the Prut in a boat once it was time to go home to the Promised Land.

While writing, I have again discovered, much to my astonishment, that I opened myself to doubt at an amazingly early age, assuring it an enclave at the heart of my faith. And only now am I becoming aware that although a candid, talkative child, I concealed many things quite naturally, as if there were no other way. As shown in other episodes, this happened for very different reasons. My great-grandfather was a naive fanatic, good-natured and weak, but irascible whenever faith seemed threatened. Furthermore, he felt called upon to defend it aggressively. My distrust of the miracle bridge would have angered and bewildered him. I didn't pretend anything; my silence was enough. He was sure I would live to see the Messiah, and he could picture me hurrying toward the paper bridge with solid steps.

I concealed many things for fear of being scolded or punished, but mostly for reasons that had to do with my developing character. Children are not the only ones who invent secrets, guarding them like enchanted treasure, using them like a cloak of invisibility, thereby—they think—keeping part of themselves inviolable. Adults often do the same without being fully aware of it. In this way, they find refuge, a protective, camouflaged isolation in the middle of their marriage or family or at work. But in my childhood, I never looked for a secret—not even in the friendships that are sealed by a secret as if by a magic cachet.

So why that bizarre silence, which not even my parents, teachers, or friends recognized or divined? Can one reject the suspicion that this child was rather unhappy? Yet nothing I have described so far would indicate an unhappy childhood. Still at this very moment, I realize I have never asked myself this question, even when my psychological writings kept pointing out that an adult's conception of childhood as the happy phase of our lives is no less absurd than the belief in a paradise that we supposedly have lost.

We know that every child experiences happiness and unhappiness almost seamlessly, that he can impulsively intensify them and just as easily lapse into indifference. This extreme intensity of experience and sudden changes eventually make it easier for memory—unconsciously tendentious—to make an adult look back at his childhood as a paradise. Actually, every child (often almost effortlessly) crosses the threshold that both separates and connects paradise and hell.

It was certainly bad luck being born in an East Galician Jewish shtetl at the turn of the century! A Jewish child had to learn how to read at the age of three, spending many hours of the day under the thumb of the strict heder teacher, learning to spell and, soon afterward, starting to translate difficult Hebrew texts. The Christian children didn't begin school until the age of six or seven. They learned how to read gradually—and only in their native tongue. And they didn't have to keep making sure not to stumble over the countless obstacles, over the do's and dont's that were vital for a child to observe as soon as he understood the words they were formulated in. So should we have envied others for not being Jewish? None of us would have even dreamed of doing that, for we were convinced that we were incomparably lucky to have been born Jews. It was wrong of the others to scorn, hate, and persecute us. But such behavior also demonstrated how unfortunate it was not to be a Jew.

On the other hand, it was, alas, true that we had to bear the misfortune of the diaspora, and that outsiders had power over us. This explained, for instance, why we spoke to our servants in their language, instead of their speaking ours. And because we lived in exile, *golus,* we had to learn two and three times as much as the others. We complained about this obligation, but it didn't make us unhappy—quite the opposite. For one thing, I came to love languages, all languages—which is why words cast as seductive a spell on the old man as they did on the child in Zablotow, who always had to find his bearings amid Ukrainian and Polish, Yiddish, Hebrew, and German. Not every language sounded beautiful, but I did feel early on that each language had something special about it, and that the world would not be the same if even one of those languages were missing. *Wasser, woda,* and *mayim* all mean the same thing, and, as I learned later, so do *acqua, eau,* and *water.* But I very soon sensed that each of these words had overtones that may not have really been inside it, but that were *evoked, aroused* by it. For me, the Slavic *woda* is drawn from a well, the Hebrew *mayim* comes gushing from a spring, and the German *wasser* pours from a faucet, which a little child can open or shut at will.

I often think of the big, powerful man who brought water to our home all year round. Each time, two full buckets, which he carried on a long pole like a yoke on his shoulders. En route to the well, he walked upright, his head high; but when he returned from the well, his neck and back were deeply bowed, heavily loaded.

Have I digressed? I wanted to talk about the happiness and unhappiness of the child that I was. Instead, I have once again evoked the water carrier. I have forgotten his name, and the features of his face are unclear now; but I have never failed to recognize how important he was for the choice of my future path. There he is in his peasant fur coat with a gigantic sheep's wool cap on his head. He slowly trudges along the icy path leading to the back of the house, where the water barrels stand. He is preceded by a grayish-white mist of the panting man's breath. Now he has arrived, he stops, he does a bizarre dance, trying to place the right-hand bucket on the ground while swiftly grabbing the yoke with both hands in order to clutch the second bucket before it tips over.

He was usually paid for one trip, that is, two buckets, or else given a lump sum for, say, a week, during which time he would supply the customer according to need. Sitting in our warm, often overheated room, we sometimes spotted him through the frosted windows; and he looked like a gigantic reeling shadow. I assumed that a man who worked so hard earned so much money that he must be the richest man in town. But if that was so, why didn't he remain in the warmth, near a high Dutch oven, and why did he drudge until late at night? I asked this question aloud at the table (we often had guests), and my question provoked loud laughter. The four-year-old's utterance was quickly circulated as an example of his childlike wisdom, not precociousness.

I was informed that the water carrier's work was hard, but so simple that anyone who had never learned a proper skill could replace him without further ado. That was why the man had to haul water from early morning until night just to make ends meet. Everyone considered it fair, even natural. But I was on the water carrier's side. And that's where I have stayed.

Another figure in Eastern Europe Jewish life impressed not only the child but also many Yiddish writers, including Yitsik-Leyb Peretz, the voice of newly discovered Hasidism and the singer of social indignation, as well as countless painters and draftsmen from shtetls in Poland, the Ukraine, White Russia, and Lithuania. Just as the bass singer has an outstanding part in a Russian chorus, so too the bassist in small bands of Jewish musicians (so-called *klezmorim*), who played chiefly at Jewish weddings but also frequently at parties given by the landed gentry. A flutist or a fiddler did not have a hard time traveling with his instruments, advancing through snow or along the muddy roads or across the loamy fields. But the bass player had to carry his instrument on his back. Arduously trudging through the snow, he and his burden, which was often larger than his body, partially covering it, resembled a gigantic black animal. In Jewish folklore, the bassist was an ambiguous and therefore strange—unsettling—figure. The starving musician, buried in a snowstorm, aroused not only pity, but also fear, like a secret messenger from a different world, an invisible and therefore all the more dangerous power. Even today, a bass solo sounds like an eerie message that I can never fully decipher.

I experienced both the worldliness of the water carrier and the spirituality of the bassist as unhappy things. But what did I experience as happy? The all-dominating faith, which determined even the slightest detail of our way of life? Yes. Yes and no. I learned early enough that it aroused the hostility of all who did not share it. So I have known since childhood that for those who nurture it, devotion is more dangerous than war or cholera. I was furious with God for repaying our devotion so poorly—even worse, for punishing instead of rewarding us. We were God's water carriers! If he were just, how could he allow much less require us to be his water carriers from eternity to eternity?

All my early doubts about God's justice, about human goodness, about myself—for skipping whole paragraphs when praying, for occasionally lying to my parents and my teacher—all these doubts could not shake my faith in the God of my ancestors. But they did diminish my confidence that the Master of the Universe, the constantly summoned *Ribono shel-Olam*, was at our side, helping us. Certainly, when the Messiah finally came some day, everything would be different, everything would be as good as good could be, and no one would need God's help. But meanwhile, life was harsh, it seemed to me, even though my brothers and I were thoroughly, even absurdly spoiled by our parents day after day.

One experience engraved itself so sharply in my memory that it has never totally slipped away or even blurred.

It happened one day during Passover Week in 1911 or, at the latest, 1912. The shtetl children had spent the morning with their fathers in the house of prayer. Now, after the festive meal, they were left to their own devices, free of any obligation, especially school—just like on the Sabbath. All at once, we noticed a peculiarly dressed man leaving the tavern. He was small and delicate, and he wore a Panama hat, a light-colored suit, and yellow shoes. In his right hand, he held a cane, playfully tossing it aloft and then catching it; but in his left hand—and this was horrible—he held a roll. The children knew he was Jewish since he lived with his mother and older sister in the beautiful *moyer* (brick house). We recognized him even though he had been away for a long time. He stood on the threshold of the tavern, so calm, so joyful, as if he hadn't just committed a terrible crime. For he had certainly drunk beer and perhaps eaten another roll, that is, leavened bread, thereby flouting the Passover laws, which are the very strictest.

The first stone hit the hand that held the roll and with which he was waving goodbye to us. A tall boy had hurled the stone; others followed his example. The man seemed astonished at first, even amused. He smiled as if to forgive a misunderstanding. But suddenly, he panicked; letting out a scream, he began to run. When the hat dropped off his head, he turned around to pick it up. At that instant, I caught up with him. I was holding a rock, but I didn't throw it, for all at once a lady in black stood between him and me. Her body shielded the terrified man who was dashing toward his home. A few steps later, she turned and said very clearly, without raising her voice: "Until the end of your lives, until your dying day, you will be ashamed that you have done this terrible thing to my sick brother." She sobbed, then fixed her eyes on me: "Tell your father what you've done. He is a just man." She sobbed again, then called me by my nickname.

I was very dejected that afternoon, and I withdrew into the darkest corner of the hay loft in case I started to cry. The tears didn't come. True, I wept seldom and briefly. I wanted to comfort myself by recalling that I didn't pick up a stone until after the tall boy did. But I felt that of all the countless *aveyres*, sins, that I had committed, this was the worst. I believed it couldn't be atoned. I still believe this today.

"*Gedenk! Erinnere dich! Tizkor!* Since earliest childhood, I had been cautioned to "remember" in three languages [Yiddish, German, Hebrew]: "Never forget any injustice done to any of your forebears. Remember the wicked things they did to others and the just punishment they suffered. Let your memory retain the good things that happened to them. Never snuff out the memory of the person who handed you a drink of water, like Rebecca, who handed the refreshing beverage to the stranger Eliezer. Whenever you set foot in the place where you did an injustice to someone else, you shall feel the woe that you were, are, shall be guilty of."

Yes, the "religion of good memory," which is followed by Erich von Stetten, a chief figure in my novels, became my religion a long time ago. It is the only religion whose commandments I make an effort to obey, even though I have my doubts, of course.

It was June 1915, a few years after that attack on the mentally disturbed young man. We were again escaping the front, which had reached our shtetl lightning-fast, some fifteen hours after the start of the new Russian offensive. The fully loaded wagon could only inch along, winding through the cannon, pontoons, and marching or riding troops, who were heading in the opposite direction, toward the battle. My father and I trudged in front of the wagon. With his right hand he calmed the horses, gently touching now one, now the other. His left hand clutched mine, which was not supposed to tremble—even when the cannon boom attacked the night with ear-splitting roars and the glow of lightning, or when the showers of the awakening morning wrapped the exhausted child in wintry cold.

That night, the shortest of the year but one of the longest in my life, a white house with beautiful steps kept appearing and reappearing before my eyes. I wanted to walk faster in order to reach those steps immediately and rest on them, perhaps even sleep for some moments with closed eyes. The image vanished as soon as we got close enough. Only the darkness remained, and the bushes. But soon, the white stair surfaced again, and behind it, the *moyer* (mansion). It was not our house, it was the home of the widow, the mother of that young innocent man, whom I had chased with a rock in my hand. His home and that of his sister (who had repeated my nickname so reproachfully) presented itself that night as a miraculous haven and then instantly fled into nothingness. I deceived myself with the apparition of that house during those hours, which were the very last hours of my childhood.

I am writing these pages in a country house. Its large French doors offer a view of seemingly manicured, custom-made forests, such as one often finds in the Île de France. Immediately adjacent to the house, there is a garden, which gently slopes down to a pasture deserted by the cows. From my window, I can see poplars right and left, completely bare now, and a young birch, which, by some miracle, has kept a few leaves on top. This tree frequently grows in the daydreams of West Europeans who originally came from Eastern Europe. At that London Congress of the Pan-Russian Social Democrats, where Lenin for once managed to rally a majority (hence the name *Bolsheviki*, majority members), the thirty-three-year-old politician as usual feverishly scrawled note after note, using a notebook page to jot down issues and demands that he hoped to bring up. But in between, he kept writing one word, always the same, though varying the script: *bryosa*, birch. It was homesickness that dictated this word to the emigré, for why else the birch right then and there?

I have penned thousands of pages, and I will probably keep on writing as long as I live. Yet I will die in the knowledge that even if I tried, in two sentences or in hundreds of sentences, I would never be able to express what trees (not just birches) and landscapes mean to me—at the very latest, since that outing with the teacher, when I learned that there is no end, or that every end is followed by many others—endlessly. . . . It is the only experience that, like life itself, is both comforting and frightening at once.

On the other hand, Zablotow and so many other Jewish shtetls have found an end. Their inhabitants were mowed down by machine guns in the marketplace or on the river bank or in the neighboring forest, or exterminated in Auschwitz, Belzec, or Treblinka. Granted, there is a village named Zablotow, inhabited by Gentiles, chiefly Ukrainians, right where our Hasidic shtetl once existed.

In my time, when the area still belonged to the Austro-Hungarian Empire, the inhabitants of the countryside were known as Ruthenians, not Ukrainians. They were mostly dirt farmers, working their wretched fields with plows to which they often hitched themselves. The good earth, the rich pastures, the teeming ponds, the forests belonged mostly to Polish aristocrats, seldom to a Jewish landowner and even more seldom to a Ruthenian. The churches were neither Roman Catholic nor Greek Orthodox, but Uniate, something in the middle, between Rome and Kiev.

The Ruthenians hated the Polish counts and barons and the imperial officials, who were almost exclusively Poles in Eastern Galicia; they also despised the Jews, who had crucified Jesus Christ and who (the Ruthenians felt), outfoxed them at the weekly markets. Yet, despite everything, there were also many, if not always easily recognizable bonds between the Jews of the shtetl and the Ruthenians. Dissimilar as they were, their shared poverty, their common technological backwardness, and finally the very different yet equally profound all-permeating faith in God brought them closer than any outsider could have guessed. Well-to-do families kept servants from the countryside—young girls as maids, young women as wet-nurses. These girls or young widows usually remained for several years, at least until they had saved enough money for trousseaux and dowries. Meanwhile, they raised the small children in the Jewish households, teaching them their first words and the beautiful songs that echoed through the Ruthenian area. The Jews admiringly quoted the proverbs of the peasants, lauding their native wit and worldly wisdom, which were even more impressive since the Ruthenians were mostly illiterate.

No, the relationship between them and us was not simple. We sensed that if they had been living in the Tsarist empire, they would have eagerly joined the pogroms. Nevertheless, we preferred them to the Poles, who monopolized the administrative and judicial systems.

Seven-year-old Havrylo was the son of a nearby farmer, who had worked in America and come home with his savings—still young enough to marry and have children, and rich enough to buy a stately farm. Instead of letting his son attend the village school, which was taught in Ruthenian, he sent him to the Polish school, which would do a better job of preparing him for secondary school. It was a long road to Zablotow, and the boy had to walk all the way, whether it was springtime or, sometimes, rainy autumn, or even winter. Havrylo would set out before dawn, and he was always the first to reach the gates of the school. Occasionally, during the long recess, he would squat down by the class-room door, out in the hallway, near the heat pipe, where he would promptly fall asleep—and be awakened just in time by the bell, not by the noise of the children.

One day a Polish boy, lured by the sleeper's vulnerability or irked by his well-groomed rustic Ruthenian clothing, called his friends over to watch him play a joke on the Ruthenian. When the ring had formed, the prankster went up to Havrylo and pissed on the back of his neck. The boy awoke, at first confused, bewildered, then he leaped up with a dreadful shriek. We, the small Jewish group, heard his terrifying yell, which was not entirely drowned out by the immediate wild laughter of the Poles, and we ran over. Perhaps I sided so vehemently (and quite uselessly) with the isolated, humiliated Havrylo, fought for him, only because a year and a half earlier I had been one of the boys who had attacked a harmless sick man who hadn't known what he was doing. But this time, I found out exactly what humiliation is and how cruel and despicable the people are who humiliate the defenseless. I discovered the baseness of the majority (by no means the only kind of baseness).

I have constantly been on the verge of asking myself whether my childhood was happy or unhappy, and I have constantly interrupted myself and gone off on a tangent. A closer look, however, reveals the obvious: so far I have described almost exclusively unhappy episodes, experiences with painful aftereffects. "What? A boy was brought up with loving care? In the middle of a shtetl of nearly proverbial poverty, he lived as if all fruits ripened for him and his kind, as if the cows filled their udders for him, the mills ground the whitest flour for him? His father's excessive trust was always there for him, encouraging him to accomplish things that made him feel superior? All this and more was given to him—and he supposedly wasn't happy?"

Well, my father's behavior had far-reaching consequences—as has already been discussed several times. But the effects were not only encouraging, for they made me a "victim of chosenness." Very few Gentiles have ever understood that Jewish suffering has become our fate not in spite of, but primarily because of, our chosenness. By making a covenant with us, God threw the divine brick of his grace on us. Ever since, we have been enduring the oppressive burden of chosenness as a curse, and yet we are supposed to praise it as a blessing three times a day.

I was never a bad son to my parents, nor was I as good a son as they deserved, for they were very good parents to their children, they couldn't have been better. My first, perhaps earliest childhood memory shows the two of them—I am only a spectator, a witness.

An unusually large, old-fashioned room with heavy brown beams, three, four, or more, sticking out out of the ceiling. It is night; I have just started out of my sleep and I see the burning candles in holders on the table, in the middle of the room. At the threshold, right under a lamp suspended from one of the beams, a lady. She throws off her coat, screams, and collapses on the bed in the corner, where my brother Meir, the second-born, the beautiful one, is lying. Now my father is next to the lady and takes her in his arms; both are weeping. I turn away, angry. *Now* she has come. I know it is too late. All three of us were sick, Meir has died. My mother was in Marienbad, she should have been here. I look at the flame on the candle; slowly, I close my eyes, leaving only a tiny slit open. Through this slit, I eagerly watch the motion of the light, which dissolves into individual rays, that come toward me, and moving dots that are alternately red and yellow. When my mother approaches my bed, I pretend to be asleep; I don't want to hear her or speak to her.

It was my father's fault, he wanted to spare my mother, so he didn't let her know the children were sick until it was too late. I understood this later. But this memory has engraved itself so sharply that I must have acted unfairly toward my mother for a long time. It was pure chance that she got to play the bad part and my father the good part. For it could easily have been different, since my parents took turns vacationing, usually each with one child.

That must have been the first time I gave in to the special delusion that provokes a child's *feeling of betrayal*. It was not until the age of nine or ten that I finally and unambiguously revised my false impression of the elegant lady who shows up only when we no longer need her, and who loudly bewails the child who had to die without her. Nevertheless, it is revealing that this memory has never changed dramaturgically, as it were. Whenever I thought back to that night, I felt sorry for my mother, not because she had lost a child, but because she had gotten into a false situation through no fault of her own. (As a psychologist and as a novelist, I have focused more on false situations and attributed more significance to them than is normally the case.)

At a very early age I learned that when I was six months old, my wet-nurse had taken advantage of my parents' absence to ransack our home with her boyfriend and run off with him that same night. Contrary to the prevailing custom of weaning children later, they had to feed me from a bottle after she left because I rejected every other breast. Whether I found out about my wet-nurse's "betrayal" before or after my brother died might be relevant for a psychological interpretation. It is possible that these two incidents caused the child to believe—consciously and unconsciously—that women could not be relied on, or at least were less reliable than men—my father, for instance.

Before I was old enough to go to school, I realized that my mother was very intelligent, indeed superior to her husband in many respects. He was generous and always loving and attentive to each of us. She always understood a child's sorrows and always did something about them in time. This may explain why, despite my two betrayal experiences, I did not mistrust women—not in my boyhood or later on. Images of disloyal women—so often depicted in folklore and all literature with ill-disguised resentment, dramatized comically and tragically—essentially reflect man's fear of woman. This usually secret, partly unconscious fear was something I certainly felt in my youth, though perhaps to a relatively minor degree—thanks to my being raised to trust people, and, second, thanks to Adler's individual psychology, of which I became a follower when I was sixteen.

In the difficult and dynamic period of adolescence with its wealth of experiences, I was still pressured by a sense of inferiority, the strongest and most durable feeling that I have suffered from since childhood—losing only gradually, step by step, the feeling of being ugly.

There are probably few people who have not experienced this sense of their own lack of worth. This fear or certainty of being unattractive or even ugly must still have a deeply discouraging effect on people of my age, any walk of life, especially women.

Lightly ironic remarks that my parents tossed off almost heedlessly must have caused my first doubts in myself. Like absolute rulers who can disseminate praise or censure without having to fear any consequences—that's how parents usually express value judgments about children, often in their presence, without realizing how heavily their foolish, mocking, half-serious words can weigh on a child's mind. The effect may last for a long time, surviving the parents' authority over the child.

In those days one of the most absurd axioms of authoritarian child rearing was that lavishing affection on a child was all right, but praise should be given rarely (to keep the child from becoming "conceited"). Thus, you had to keep a child from knowing he was intelligent. If, however, he let on that he realized he was intelligent, then you reproached him for being conceited. When such attempts were made on me, I defended myself, not without success, by arguing, "You want me to be smart enough so that other people notice, but stupid enough so that I am the only one who doesn't know I'm smart."

However, I felt helpless about being ugly. This stopped completely when I became indifferent to my appearance—non-existent, so to speak. However, this happened much later, long after my parents had explained that it was all a misunderstanding, an unexpected misinterpretation. They reminded me of all the nicknames they had given me, emphasizing my special qualities: my thick black hair, which fell down to my shoulders in long curls, my radiant gaze, the expression on my face . . . . How was it possible, they asked me, that I hadn't sensed something else beyond their mocking words—the pride with which they spoke about me?

And it is true; a very young child in a Jewish shtetl learned that the intonation is more meaningful than the words. He could distinguish at an early age whether the expression, "Oy, is she ever beautiful!" meant that a girl was indeed very lovely or terribly ugly. I think can remember how astonished, how bewildered I was to discover that a word could also mean its opposite. But soon I noticed, to my satisfaction, that, like all the rest of us, I had no trouble catching the proper drift, figuring out whether "Oy, what a philosopher!" referred to a sage or a moron.

In the Jardin du Luxembourg, the gardeners are busy removing the final weary autumn flowers from the beds, piling up the dry leaves in huge heaps along the paths. Now that the trees are so bare, it is hard to picture their recent past and imminent future. Here and there, a few leaves, some not even yellow, hang at the extreme tips of branches. One of the many permanent goals of my daily wanderings through this park is now—but for how many more days?—some lonesome leaf, still intact, on a branch. It may sound silly, but whenever I find one of these leaves, I feel as much pleasure as if I had suddenly received a gift I had done nothing to deserve.

"He spoke about a tree that had almost miraculously remained standing between the enemy trenches. About the leaf, a single leaf still attached to the branch. He worried about it when the winds became too vehement. And the joy of finding it again the next morning!"

This comes from a letter that a very young volunteer in World War I writes to his father from the Italian front. Nothing has remained of his enthusiasm for the Fatherland, the war, and the sublime goals—nothing, not even a concept—merely an endangered field of vision encompassing things that are almost as greatly menaced as the human lives—among them, the last leaf.

On the terraces surrounding the fountain in an oval curve, I see the stone queens and princesses of France, standing guard to protect themselves from each other in summer and winter. Some of them look as if they had been frequently deceived and rejected by their spouses and lovers, and the others as if they had always been trying to think of a way of getting rid of their men. In these dreary morning hours, when the few pedestrians hurry across the park, I am often the only stroller to stop in front of these stone figures and gaze up at their blank faces. I involve them in a game I have played since adolescence: making up the character and destiny, sometimes an entire biography, of people who remain in my field of vision for a while: people sitting across from me in a train compartment, waiting in the same room with me to watch a film or board an airplane. These people are always en route. ("Underway," "The Useless Journey," "The Futile Return," "Without End" are titles I have used for some sections of my novels.)

Not far from the rather successful statue of Marie de Medici, a Florentine banker's fat daughter who had this palace and garden built after murdering her husband, there is a monument that is seldom noticed. A very low, gray pyramid rises, almost indistinct, over a narrow rectangular bed, where small yellow flowers are planted during the warm season, decorating the square tombstone with a cross and two daggers carved in the center. Above them, there is a small bronze relief depicting a young person who seems to be grieving. I don't recall ever seeing a stroller pause at this memorial. One practically has to stumble over it to notice it: amid the floral wealth of the garden, these small yellow blossoms would attract no one, even if they were placed more effectively.

So I am probably the only visitor to direct his steps toward this memorial, which stirs no one's mind, even though the highly legible engraved inscription might give one food for thought and awaken memories in older people: *"Ici / sept héros / de la résistance / ont été fusillés / par les Allemands / le 19 Août 1944"* * Almost every day, I spend a moment in this place where these seven men—two municipal policemen and five volunteers, all probably very young—had to die three decades ago. Had to? Why, for what purpose? The Germans were already hurriedly evacuating the city; these seven men and others like them could not accelerate this operation, nor did they have to try. The Wehrmacht, for its part, would not have lost the war one minute earlier, had it let these seven prisoners go or sent them to a stalag.

My frequent visits to this execution site have less to do with the past and my memories than with the topography: right behind this area is the *Boulodrome,* the fenced-in bowling green where the players spend hours playing *boule.* This game, especially popular in the south of France among men of all classes, always draws spectators. I became one of them some time ago, ever since I stopped playing myself. On weekdays the players are all elderly men. They arrive late in the morning and in the afternoon, even in cold weather, and two, four, or six of them play several games without passion but with steady intensity.

One or another of the seven victims, who had probably all lived in this district, could have been one of the *boulistes.* Paris, France, the world—no one needed their presence in this spot during those August days. And even if I finally managed to memorize their names, this would not guarantee their share of the immortality so frivolously promised to these heroes.

"You know it too, Lagrange, that look in the eyes of young men who are trying to find someone who makes them want to sacrifice themselves. I flee them like the plague. There is an off-season for animals in the woods. Off-season, Lagrange, for these young men!"

These words are spoken in the summer of 1941 (three years before these seven were shot) by Doino Faber, a central figure in my novels, a "battle-weary revolutionary," who hopes he will finally succeed in filling himself "with the dry sand of indifference." During that same conversation, he declares:

"No, I do not deny the past, but I find what I have done super-

* (Here, seven heroes of the Resistance were shot by the Germans on August 19, 1944.)

fluous . . . a waste of time, a waste of energy. It would have been better if I had played bowls every day, and it would certainly have made more sense."

Perhaps the boulistes look out for me, the attentive but silent spectator, if I have not shown up for several days. They don't mind having someone witness their triumphs, and we conduct a wordless dialogue. But I would have asked an off-season for the seven dead men and the right to play bowls instead of their heroic interference with history, which did not need them. Yet these seven remain silent in the monologue of a stroller who, because he still hasn't been able to fill himself "with the dry sand of indifference," finds it increasingly unbearable that young men are seduced or forced into sacrificial murder and sacrificial death. The sixty-seven-year-old man still hasn't succeeded in living as if they and their kind had never existed, as if they still didn't exist everywhere.

Whether I linger by the bouloudrome or by the half-secret monument, by the basin on which the tiny caravels still reach the shore despite the whirlpool caused by the fountain, or by the carousel whose does, lions, elephants, and white horses were described with friendly exaggeration by Rainer Maria Rilke—no matter where, I keep thinking of the memoirs that I have begun to write, not without qualms and hesitation. A man who adheres as closely to the present as I do, who is so concerned with, bothered by, annoyed at—or, on rare occasions, enthusiastic about—current events will always see the past in terms of the present. Yet I experience the present moment in the light and shadow of the past, of previous experiences, whether or not they are actually comparable.

For several weeks now, it has been harsh, naked winter in this garden—the very last leaves are gone, they burned quickly. Twigs and branches look gray in the stingy light of these short winter days. Occasionally, it seems about to snow. Now and then, for a few minutes, a few gray flakes fall in thin wisps to the gray ground. Sometimes I feel sorry for them, as I did for the old beggars who used to sing in the back courts of our street in Vienna. One of them usually broke off after the first stanza, declaring dramatically, "Let's not pretend. I don't have a voice anymore, and I don't have the strength to sing. So throw down your donations and I'll stop bothering you with my croaking!"

The old man (he was probably a lot younger than I am today) and a hundred others suddenly stand before me; I run across them on all the roads I have ever taken. Then they sink back into the darkness. They keep appearing because I open my notebook every day, not putting it aside until I have written at least two pages. Writing has revived those old anxieties that afflicted me in my childhood, when I was worried about being ugly. My memory of that suffering is vivid, but the thought of those completely unknown young men who lost their lives much too prematurely and senselessly haunts me even more intensely. The event of August 19, 1944 contains nearly all the elements of the challenge that has prevented me—since the First World War, when I was ten—from being politically indifferent. In retrospect, I think that such incidents as the persecution of the young madman at Passover or the humiliation of the Ukrainian boy at school must have influenced my behavior and the choice of my battle positions more strongly than any sense of inferiority about my ugliness. But what if this feeling aroused my hypersensitivity, making me experience those really quite trivial incidents with such painful commiseration that they are still vivid in my mind today?

In my childhood, being ugly seemed both undeserved and inescapable. Still, one could hope to look tolerable, perhaps even attractive— not just by *being,* the way beautiful people could, but by *doing.* I probably didn't envy anyone for his beauty, since my father's overestimation—and his always encouraging if oppressively exorbitant demands—made me feel confident that I did have some value. And I must have discovered very early that sensitivity to beauty is a special gift. Even as an infant I was exhilarated by the beauty of the snowy world, the frost flowers on the window panes, the hoar on the twigs. Grateful for this capacity, I will probably appreciate beauty actively until the end of my life. In my mind I have written countless letters of gratitude to writers, painters, and actors, and I still do so today. But these letters are only imagined—perhaps partly out of timidity, but also, oddly enough, because once you have thought out every last detail of the letter you want to write, there is less need to actually commit it to paper. Thus, the intention replaces its realization, which vanishes into the imaginary graveyard of stillborn deeds.

I remember the first face whose beauty I admired so immensely that I was very timid, even dumbstruck for several minutes. It was the face of a boy who, together with his family, visited our shtetl for only a few days. He and his sister were dressed exotically and elegantly in silk and velvet—like a prince and a princess, people said. That afternoon I heard the word *dove-gray* for the first time—the color of his clothes. His brow curved very lightly under his parted chestnut hair, and the white of his forehead contrasted with his dark eyes and the shiny tone of his cheeks.

The boy had a not too conspicuous but visible hump. You avoided—no, you instantly forgot about the hump once you had fixed your eyes on the visitor's face.

My vivid memory of this meeting may be due to the fact that for many years I kept thinking about it. Probably for several reasons. Their beauty, enhanced by a truly surprising elegance, fit the petit-bourgeois ideal to a T; it corresponded to an aesthetics shaped by the third estate, true to its desire to resemble the aristocracy (which it had replaced) in both appearance and expression. Had I known Murillo's street urchins at that time, I wouldn't have found them appealing, because they are utterly inconsistent with the middle-class image of "nobility."

Is it conceivable that a child of five or six reacted almost instinctively in terms of "class"? Undoubtedly. Wherever poverty and destitution characterize the living conditions of an overwhelming majority, the social and economic differences, no matter how minor, penetrate each person's consciousness indelibly. From an early age, I heard derogatory if not scornful remarks about the "common people," "mob," "hoi polloi," "ignorant," "peasant yokels," and even about certain less skillful craftsmen. In contrast, people praised anything and anyone considered "fine," which was synonymous with anything desirable—the so-called noble, or ideal.

My feeling of ugliness was reinforced continuously by my "peasant-like" appearance. I had long, black hair; my nose did not have a sharp, thin bridge; and my eyes were dark and prominent instead of subdued. "Cossack" was one of my nicknames, which meant partly that my looks were not "fine" enough.

Did I become so interested in Alfred Adler's individual psychology some ten years later because it assigns an enormously important role to the sense of inferiority? Perhaps—but since hardly any human being in possession of his faculties has escaped the burden of this feeling, everyone would be irresistibly drawn to Adler's teachings if this were the only reason. Yet we know that this emphasis is not the attraction, since the term "inferiority complex" actually makes many people uncomfortably deprived and debased. Adler won me over, I think, because he stressed the determination and courage to overcome difficulties, including a sense of inferiority. Thus, everything I say about my suffering as a child is meaningful only if that suffering is also understood as providing incentive to overcome it. In my childhood, I felt despair more frequently during childhood than in later years; and even as a child I sensed that despair is usually the impatience of a hopeful man.

Today when I endure my impatience (that of an elderly man) only reluctantly, often with seething resentment, I think back to the people the child compared himself with to observe, criticize, and condemn himself—that is, to gauge what he viewed as his excessively slow development and activity. When I started thinking of myself as inadequate, my compensatory behavior began. It led quite often to real achievement, genuinely overcoming obstacles, but also to shadow-boxing, deceptions, and self-deceptions: the usual game of lies, the "as-if" fictions. I was both spectator and actor in this farce—a cheated boy who fooled the cheater, for he merely pretended not to know that he had been taken in. I admired Berele, but by no means did I want to be like him. I immensely admired the conjurer who spirited colored cloths from nowhere and instantly made them vanish again. But I did not want to be like him either, for I knew that everything was a *comedy*. We children used the Yiddish word *komedye* loosely: it meant putting on an act, fooling around, but also playing a nasty prank, like tricking someone into thinking that the neighbor's cow had flown over the house and laid an egg on the roof. Such a victim, we said in the shtetl, could believe anything under the sun: *nisht geshtoygn nisht gefloygn*. (We also used the idiom "you lie like a rug" whenever we caught someone telling a fib.)

I must have experienced at a very early age the seductiveness of my own imagination and yielded almost unresistingly. Imagination filled the gaps between facts; even more often, it replaced the child's missing knowledge. "One really should know . . ." I frequently said to myself— and still do, when I hear information so lacking in essential data that it does not allow you to form an opinion or reach a conclusion about the course of events. The adult waits with controlled impatience, the child did not wait. His imagination swiftly filled in the terra incognita, connecting it with familiar reality, so that imagination and perception were united.

From the ages of four to seven, perhaps even eight, I saw myself as a liar, a child who lied more than the others but was lucky enough to be found out and punished less often than he deserved. For several months, my teacher was an extremely poor man known as Shmerl the Blindman. He, his wife, his many children, and his old mother shared a room with the poultry. In that room the pupils, squeezed together on rickety benches, learned to read in chorus. I was miserable when Shmerl was my teacher; furthermore, I couldn't stand the smells in the room, which got worse every day, or the glare of his mother's red-rimmed eyes, which looked alarmingly like those of the annoying chickens. I tried to run away several times and was brought back immediately. Then something awful happened: I made in my pants. The teacher instantly sent me home. During the brief period that I was forced to study with Shmerl, I didn't have to run away anymore. I merely stood in front of him with my legs apart and confessed that I had had another "accident." I was then free for the rest of the day. That was how I discovered something that stood me in good stead for several years. All one had to do was feign certain chiefly nervous ailments, which was what my incontinence must have been, and one could reap the advantages normally supplied only by a real illness. This discovery must have been made by countless children, especially those who are unhappy in school. But it gave me food for thought, leading me deviously and circuitously to insights that would be important for my development.

The countless repeated successes of the "as if" that I faked for Shmerl the Blindman both impressed and dismayed me: the wall between true and false, between reality and apperance seemed to topple as soon as you gave free rein to your imagination. I can't guess what I knew about imagination back then or what I merely had an inkling of, but I am sure the three-year-old child had already realized that the imagination points the way to freedom. Since then, this faculty, which may more aptly be called "realistic fantasy," has played a dominant role in my thoughts, in my decisions and actions, and in my work as a writer. And it has been just as useful to the psychologist as to the novelist.

My lies caused me no remorse, only anxiety. If I kept deviating more and more from the truth, would I eventually become incapable of distinguishing it from falsehood? If I heard about an event, I would embroider it as soon as I was alone, just before falling asleep or right after waking up. I expanded on the time and place of the action, made up details and let them seduce me into concocting a narrative. Initially, I felt I was simply clarifying what I had heard, but actually I was supplying a shape—molds that I had to fill. When I began writing novels, I almost always embellished episodic figures with biographical details that I omitted from the final version because the embellishments were not only unnecessary but detrimental to the overall structure. Even now when I write, I cannot help thinking up life stories that I never even set down since they would obviously be out of place.

A man suddenly appeared in the street. He wore shirtsleeves even though it was cold out, and he was running as if he were fleeing someone. Never looking back, he gesticulated, signalling someone, but there was no one to be seen. All at once he halted, slowly turned around, and made a fist almost playfully, humorously; we could not see whomever he was threatening. I happened to be standing outside our house witnessing this strange, mute scene. Had I been curious about the "real" facts, I could easily have found out what was going on with this stranger—why he was fleeing and threatening at the same time. But instead of inquiring, I began to concoct and fill in. If someone had asked me about the incident, I would have served up a story with a beginning and an end; if he had also pressed me about my source, I would have replied: "I don't know, I just think that's what happened." I never lost sight of the boundary between experience and fantasy, but I did what I had to in order to make that line fluid and, eventually, invisible.

Another reason I viewed myself as a liar was that I never made up a wholly unbelievable story and very seldom invented even an improbable one. In contrast, one could always expect the interference in the action by invisible forces in fairy tales. But the only stories that scared me were those in which real wild beasts attacked people. I have never been afraid of witches or any other creature with a human face in these tales that were often creepy. Thus my insertions, connecting the fragments in which reality presented itself to me, were never fantastic, they were always realistic or—shall we say—probable.

What was it that gave me the unsettling certainty at such an early age that everything was only a fragment and that the goal was to see the "hills behind the hills," climb them, and never forget that they exist—and that you will know next to nothing if you lose sight of them. Another metaphor that impressed me at an early age: A long, rolled-up object sits there; you kick it, and it starts moving, unrolling; it is a long, wide carpet with many colored patterns, which may signify only themselves, but probably signify a lot more—namely, pieces of news, wise sayings, credos, or accounts of mysterious events.

Anything that exists may survive for a long time or perish quickly; but much of what exists signifies much more than it appears to be, because it is rolled up or folded up. "Ve ani" ("And I . . .") are the opening words of one of the many sentences with which the dying Jacob announces his last will and very last wishes to Joseph and his other sons. In thousands of one-room schools, during the same week, Jewish children learned how to translate that biblical passage with its commentary. And for countless generations, these children had been repeating the text handed down orally, with its singsong: "And I Jacob, who ask of thee that thou bury me not here, in foreign soil, but in Meúrat Hamakpela, in the land of Canaan. I did not do likewise for thy mother. I buried her by the side of the road, right where she died. No, it was not far from Padan, where I could have buried her, and the roads were not impassable but dry, like a sieve in the sun. Why did I not bring her corpse to Padan? Because the time will come when the nation of Israel, conquered and despairing, will take this road into exile. And Rachel will rise from her grave on the wayside, she will bless her children and lift the spirits of the afflicted. . . ." Yes, this and a great deal more was contained in the unspoken words accompanying the beginning of the sentence "And I. . . ."

I considered myself a liar also because I often gave in to an urge to make up things that could have happened but hadn't, relating them as if they had come from a reliable source or, much more rarely, as if I had witnessed them personally.

Naturally, like so many children, I also lied freely, to conceal some omission on my part or justify some wrongdoing; and I often lied in order to escape the boredom of verbose prayers. I figured that since God is omniscient, I couldn't deceive *him*; besides, since he was omnipotent, he couldn't have cared about a few prayers more or less.

Between my eighth and ninth year a change occurred: I frequently felt offended, degraded by my own lies, even when they weren't exposed. In spite of all my efforts to remember what caused this change, I have not been able to come up with a reason for it. But suddenly the lies made me unhappy, like a drunk who awakens, sober, to find himself lying in filth after a night of boozing, and who suddenly realizes how despicable his companions are. I don't think I instantly resolved never to lie again— that resolution would have quickly wavered anyway. (I already knew the final verse of a psalm often repeated in the liturgy: "Every man lies.") However, I did begin to watch myself, first with little, then with increasing success.

A certainly unforeseen side effect of my new rigorousness became important in the course of time: early on, the boy's critical attitude toward anything ungenuine, expressed in words, looks, or gestures, intensified his need for the genuine. And from that time on, I developed my ability to make increasingly clear distinctions between fiction and reality. Life was often very sad, but it offered more than enough basis and material for *komedye*. At twelve or thirteen I thought I would not play "comedy" anymore. I was wrong, and my mistake was almost as unavoidable as the human comedy itself.

On one afternoon around that time, probably early spring 1914, a well-dressed stranger, carrying the kind of satchels used by traveling salesmen, collapsed in the middle of the street, near our home. People gathered around; they didn't know how to help him. Finally, they brought him to our home. They placed him on a couch, opened his collar, held smelling salts under his nose, and poured a glassful of liquor into his mouth as he gasped for breath. He quickly came to, and replied readily if tersely to the questions asked by the doctor, who had hurried over. The stranger explained that he hadn't eaten for two days because he had had only enough money to pay for his night's lodging at the inn. His business trip had been completely useless and unsuccessful, and now he didn't even have enough money for a railroad ticket back home. While he was enjoying the meal, which was as good as any medicine, a collection was taken up. One hour later, the man started off again, just in time to catch his train.

That evening the incident, which had excited everyone, was discussed in our home. Although no one said so outright, it was obvious that they all believed the man's collapse in the street, in an expediently chosen place, was a well-executed sham. The man had really been in despair, he had really not eaten, and it had become too hard for him to keep lugging his old-fashioned, unsellable shoes. Those were all good reasons, people admitted, but they hinted that he had pretended to faint in order to succeed in obtaining food and cash, more money than he needed for the train ticket, and finally sympathy—Jewish commiseration, they said, so lavishly donated and so often misspent.

Before they passed from hesitant irony to open sarcasm about an unfortunate stranger, my father cut in. The point was, he said, that the man really needed help and wouldn't have gotten it quickly and abundantly if he hadn't fainted in broad daylight to attract everyone's attention.

The incident itself might not have been so interesting to me, except for its long-lasting significance: You can express the truth, even present it more convincingly, by shrewd pretense—by concocting something that isn't wholly genuine. The traveling salesman had been weak from hunger that day, he didn't have a penny in his pocket, and he would have had to beg for days in order to scrape his train fare together. That was why his fainting spell was the best and probably only method for saving himself and preventing the shtetl from sharing the responsibility for his imminent misfortune.

Yes, that was how it was—and I grasped this partly because that was how my father explained it. At the same time, I was as deeply affected as if it had happened directly to me. That so intentional, so expedient blend of facts and contrivance had been successfully presented as true—I had been guilty of that myself, not only when I wanted to get away from Shmerl the Blindman and the eyes of the old woman. But now, listening to the ironic commentary by the adults, I suddenly realized that although the salesman's success was undeniable, it was humiliating, a disgrace—and that no benefit is worth humiliation. The eight-year-old came to the conclusion partly because his father, without realizing it, had kept feeding the child's pride.

One reason we needed to feel pride was that all of us in the shtetl keenly felt the hatred of the anti-Semites—the same hatred that had been used for thousands of years to justify anti-Semitic attitudes. They came up with new rationales every day. During the second decade of this century, Jewish assimilationists, trying to blur their identity through baptism or extreme self-denial, were escaping not so much the disadvantages of being Jewish as the scorn of the Jew-baiters. They eventually gave in uninhibitedly to the compulsion to debase their fellow Jews and, secretly, themselves. At the same time, Jews, especially in Central and Eastern Europe, developed a new sense of identity and thereby a new self-esteem. It no longer sufficed to ignore the hate-mongers; one had to beat them back, fight them, as Jewish self-defense groups were already doing occasionally, taking arms against the pogrom mobs and their Czarist ringleaders.

Every person's self-esteem is tested thousands of times throughout his life. But for people like me, this feeling was also determined by how deeply each one individually felt about being Jewish: as ignominy or as honorable loyalty, as a condition caused by a fluke of birth or as a task, namely, to live as if bearing responsibility for the others. The person who despised himself could not carry out this mission; therefore a Jew had to try to keep up his self-esteem every day, never jeopardizing it for any reason.

That shoe salesman had resorted to cunning; well, cunning was despicable. That's what I felt then for the first time, with an intensity that would never abate. Even today, the most successful cunning strikes me as the calculation of stupid or hopelessly narrow-minded people. I had admired Berele, who was cunning, and felt grateful to him for playing a *komedye* for me, which I was delighted to see through every day. But now

I was way beyond that—I ordered myself not to lie and took no pleasure in other people's ruses and tricks. I even believed that Berele had debased himself and had tricked me into humiliating him. Of course, I still fibbed occasionally, but I supervised myself with that special childhood severity which most adults have forgotten. I became cross with myself whenever I heard myself (for no solid reason and with no sensible aim—just on impulse, carried away by my narrative zeal) mingling experience and fiction so thoroughly that I thought the ground under my feet would give way. As I have said, this had come about because my fictions were neither pipe dreams nor boasts nor harmless fantasies—they dovetailed with reality. I nearly always made up something that could actually have happened. (We all know the device that at one time was often used by writers: waiting until the end of a tale to reveal in the final paragraph that what they have realistically rendered was actually a dream. In other cases, the author claimed that he was repeating a story told to him by a stranger he had happened to meet at a lonesome inn, or that he was sharing the contents of a manuscript he had found in an attic.

I resolved henceforth to divide reality neatly, distinguishing actual events from those that were merely possible or probable. I succeeded only to some degree. At seventeen I felt an almost irresistible urge to write stories and novels. I wrote a little but soon gave up because I wanted to devote all my time to psychology—and did so until the age of thirty-five, when I began concentrating on literature. And that was what happened, although somewhat later than I had planned. An activity that I ordered myself to abstain from as a child, so that I would not be a liar, eventually became my profession. As a novelist, I combined real events with *infinite possibility*, giving the latter a special kind of reality.

No, I was never really a liar as a child, though at times I believed that I was or could become one. I have not become fanatical about telling the truth, at least not in my daily dealings with other people. Molière's Alceste, the misanthrope, is not an ethical model but an annoying fool, an extremely clumsy bore who uses truth like a sledgehammer. Such fanatical devotion to truth does not serve truth; it merely promotes inane exaggerations of reality, a tendency to put down other people and establish one's own superiority.

Even on the coldest days in the Luxembourg gardens, I come upon large groups of children, in class, doing an hour of sports with their teachers. I see large and small clusters forming, a few loners going off on

their own, other pupils so deeply involved in converations that they seem
oblivious to the sometimes deafening noise. Today from my park bench I
observed two grade-school pupils, hardly more than eight years old and
roughly the same size. A melancholy pensiveness written on their faces
reflected the boys' intensity. One boy, who had black curls and very
handsome clothes, spoke almost without stopping. His head was lowered,
and he raised it only when the other boy interrupted him with an answer.
Naturally, I tried to guess or make up what they were talking about.
Whatever it was, it wouldn't have affected me as much as the arresting
earnestness of their bearing. Yes, I told myself, I ought to write about
that, about the fact that whatever may be weighing on a child's mind, he
usually feels it much more strongly than an adult does. Grief, expectation, anxiety, joy and depression—a child always commits himself entirely. Everything seems final, but it quickly flashes by, replaced almost
without transition by a different feeling, which feels just as *fleetingly final.*

I stared at the two boys; in a virtually retrospective premonition I
empathized with now one boy, then the other, and felt like following
them when they eventually left the park with their classmates. I remained seated, suddenly unnerved, doubting whether I could ever succeed in evoking my own childhood and bringing it home, palpably close,
to the reader.

What did I care about that child, the boy who was eight years old
almost six decades ago? In 1915 all our family photos were destroyed by
Cossacks who plundered the house and remained there for several days.
The images revived by my memory probably come from those pho-
tographs. All of them showed me in festive garb; in several I was near my
brother, who was three and a half years older, and a few showed me in a
group portrait. There were five of us, for my little brother, five and a half
years younger, was also present. In those days, I was often accused of
looking both defiant and sad. Sad was almost a compliment, because
melancholy was viewed as a sign of more noble humanity—at least in the
shtetl, which, like any provincial town, was years behind the prevailing
spirit of the times.

I recall that boy with genuine curiosity, but I do not feel attached to
him in any way; I am not he, and if I am his child, then he was never my
father.

My vanity does not leave me, and it will probably fade only with my
last breath; but he was even more vain than I am. Not only because he
was afraid of disappointing people, but because he was so bent on

pleasing them—not everyone, of course. Hence his defiant gaze; he didn't care what the photographer thought of him. The boy was saddened only by the realization that he was totally unlike his blond brother, who took after their beautiful mother. I must have envied my brother, although I don't exactly remember. But I do know that I was often annoyed, even bitter, that he, as the firstborn, and my younger brother, as the youngest, were given privileges that had always been withheld from me (or so I thought)—and only because, through no fault of my own, I had been unlucky enough to be born between them. I felt envious and slighted—each two feelings increasing the other—but in the child's consciousness, as in the minds of so many people who were the "middle child," the chief source of suffering was moral indignation at the injustice of the situation.

Even before I became lodged in the "sandwich position," that is, when I was still the younger of two sons, my behavior was determined by extreme sensitivity toward any kind of injustice even more than any piety. For instance, when I could finally tie my own shoes, I tried to find some way of not disadvantaging either shoe. If I pulled my right shoe on first, I tied the left one first, for justice' sake. I also made a point of alternating right and left. This was not due to any anthropomorphizing fantasy. At stake was not the object, but the person—I myself. One always had to make sure that one wasn't unjust to anyone.

Yosher: this Hebrew word signified not only "justice," but also "just magnanimity." The goal was not punishment, but generous, magnanimous reparation. And this was always inspired by a principle that Judaism was the first to formulate and make practicable: the equality of human beings before God, i.e., equal rights and equal laws for everyone at all times.

In everything I heard as a small child and learned and read later on, people spoke about the blasphemous arrogance with which the wealthy and powerful bent the law so that the poor and powerless helplessly suffered injustice. And long before I learned how to translate the words of the prophet Isaiah, I knew that injustice would vanish from the earth only after the coming of the Messiah. In the meantime, however, no one was permitted to witness an injustice passively, even if he had absolutely no connection with the misdeed, the perpetrator, or the victim. I was no roughneck, but I still got into fights when I believed I had to side with a child who was the underdog, or was insulted in some way, or attacked for no reason. And if I arrived home afterward in a somewhat battered state,

I was never reprimanded, for my parents considered it proper—no, necessary—for me to intervene, especially since I was tall for my age and, although very thin, rather strong.

My father was known as a man of yosher, and people often asked him to act as judge in bitter quarrels that tore close relatives, whole families, or old friends apart. My father allowed me to be present when he, aided by two "assessors," presided over these cases, whether the issue was a mere bagatelle, property (usually some miserable heirlooms), a breach or annulment of contract, or any kind of injury. At times, I barely understood the verbose complaints and accusations, but I was often fascinated by the alarming, even shattering intensity of the hate-filled alienation expressed during many of these proceedings. And the alienation, as I eventually realized, was almost always caused by frustrated hopes, betrayal of trust, or disappointment in love.

As was written in the first chapter of Genesis, God began the creation of the world by forever separating light and darkness, day and night. The words signified not only their literal meaning but, like most portions of the Bible, much more. Each level had sublevels, if not abysses, in which one had to discover a second, a third meaning. Right and wrong, just like day and night, were separate from each other, unmistakably distinct and irreconcilable.

The boy sitting in the corner of the large room listening to the charges and countercharges sometimes feared becoming the helpless victim of a paralyzing confusion. Everything was so tangled up that cause and effect seemed to chase one another in a circle, eventually becoming indistinct from each other. A number of these trials had such profound impact on me that I can still feel their indirect influence today.

Three families were involved in an extremely violent dispute. Daughter A, already twenty-four years old, the eldest of four sisters, was engaged to B. Several months before the wedding date, her father died unexpectedly, leaving the family, as it turned out, in such complete financial ruin that it was uncertain whether the widow could come up with the promised dowry. Family C now began scheming, trying to get B to break off the engagement and marry their own daughter. It was bruited about that A had caught tuberculosis from her father, who supposedly had been carried off by galloping consumption. This false rumor, maliciously spread, was bound to have disastrous consequences for the dead man's family, since shtetl Jews feared consumption almost more than epilepsy or even madness. B did not instantly terminate his engagement;

he stalled and kept putting off the wedding, demanding that the dowry be deposited immediately with one of his relatives. And everyone knew, of course, that he was already frequenting the C home.

B, a smug young man with a waxed mustache and a fashionable Vandyke, could not be talked into making a firm decision. He was not intelligent, just a slightly cunning simpleton, and he continued to be evasive about answering; whenever he did finally come out with an answer, he would immediately take it back. The court had to convene several times but failed to reach any verdict. About six months later, B married the girl from family C.

It was probably because of this trial that, ever since my childhood, I have always felt sorry for girls left on the shelf; I pity them whether I encounter them in real life or in books and movies. I picture them as women who experience their status as a daily humiliation and try to escape it by indulging in often unfounded hopes, whose abrupt end always arouses a senseless indignation and finally an immobilizing depression.

The inhabitants of the shtetl, like those of other small communities, knew virtually everything about everyone, and they were especially interested in supposedly well-kept secrets. If you looked at a girl who was thought to have "missed the boat" or might easily become a spinster, you could tell at a glance whether she had any reason to keep hoping if, for example, she got all dressed up on an ordinary weekday. Perhaps she expected a visitor, a *shadkhen* (marriage broker), or even a suitor, since every single man between twenty and sixty was considered an eligible bachelor in Zablotow. Or she might stride proudly across the village square to remind a former suitor of her existence or to challenge more successful rivals.

Whatever it was, the sight of an unmarried older girl always saddened me, even if I found her attractive and would have liked her to speak to me. I remember one such girl: her name was Leah, but she only wanted to be called Lotte, from Goethe's *Werther*, of course. She would have long conversations with me; the longest were about our shtetl, which she despised. On good days, she was convinced she wouldn't remain here much longer: she would marry a man from a big city, probably Vienna, and move there. At times, when her despair made her want to die as soon as possible, she would ply me with questions about what I wanted to be and where and how I would live. It was as if she were trying to escape her own unbearable present and seek refuge in the boy's future, which she thought she could foresee very accurately. From her reading, she knew all about the "grand life" in Vienna, Venice, Paris, Ostend, Monte Carlo. . . . At the mere sound of these names, her cheeks turned rosy again; she forgot that she wanted to die right away and was happy to arrange my future "grand life."

Sometimes she let me do small favors for her: buy her something in the pharmacy, the dry goods store, the delicatessen—some item that she needed right away but didn't want to shop for herself, because she didn't want to give her female enemies the satisfaction of seeing her unwashed and ugly.

One reason I liked Leah/Lotte was certainly because she clearly let me know that she liked me, and because she sometimes listened to me as if she had been waiting for my words since time immemorial. Furthermore, I had such deep, strangely mixed emotions about her that sometimes I had to look away, so she wouldn't notice what she aroused in me. It wasn't so much she herself as the sometimes almost unbearable intensity of her expectation—her desperate, overpowering, impatient hope and disquiet—that always overwhelmed her with such inescapable impact whenever a "decisive moment" again seemed imminent, when happiness stopped at her door. But, she used to lament, it never came in.

As I write, I try to recall the features of her face but am unable to do so; her gestures, however, are still as vivid as if I had only just observed them. She would always keep tossing her head back to flip one of her braids from her shoulder to her back. This motion was accompanied by an imperious expression, as if she were trying to get her way with a recalcitrant servant. She was intent on having a "floating" gait; that was why she put weight on her heel as seldom as possible—she practically tiptoed. But when she felt sad and discouraged, she collapsed, and her feet dragged along slowly.

Leah was moody. Breaking off in mid-sentence, even during the liveliest conversations, she could leave me without even saying goodbye, which usually hurt me so deeply that I resolved to avoid her. But she didn't have to make much of an effort to win me back. How much I forgave her! Yet there was one thing I didn't forgive—the degrading misery she jumped into with wide-open eyes.

The young man was named Max. He always sported the latest fashion and had neither a beard nor a mustache, much less sidelocks, of course. The shtetl Jews said he was the "natural son" of a stranger—perhaps a rich man—and a very young widow who had returned to

Zablotow when the child was ten years old. Her "fashion salon" didn't bring in much, but she certainly wasn't dependent on it, they said, because she was supported generously, probably by her ex-lover. Max, by no means stupid, did not want to go to school—certainly not in this "godforsaken dump" his mother had brought him to. He was a jack-of-all-trades and a prankster, who invited himself everywhere and was never thrown out because he entertained everyone with his jokes, wisecracks, unsettling suggestiveness, and exciting rumors that occasionally turned out to be true. People never forgot that he was a "bastard," and they despised him for being uneducated and a passionate cardplayer who lost far too seldom. He had a ruddy, freckled face that always seemed to be laughing—laughing at you, deriding you. But if you looked closer, there was no cheer in his eyes, and they seemed to be prying.

I avoided Leah. When I saw her from afar, I took detours. She was throwing herself away, they said; I agreed and I was angry with her. She, for her part, no longer needed to confide in me, yet she spoke to me several times whenever she popped up so unexpectedly that I couldn't avoid the encounter. I normally remained silent. Once, though, she ran after me, grabbed my shoulder, and whispered, "Some day, you'll understand, some day. I'm going away. Forever. When I'm gone, stop being angry at me. And if ever you write books, like Karl Emil Franzos, for instance, think of me! But don't call me Leah, call me Lotte, only Lotte!"

Yesterday I wanted to add a concluding sentence: "I don't remember ever hearing from her again; I certainly never ran into her again." I was about to set it down when I began to wonder: What? Why had my memory retained that episode in such detail? When had I last thought of Leah? Ten years ago, thirty, fifty? I don't know. Perhaps I didn't wrest this episode from oblivion—I may have invented it while writing.

In the Zablotow of today, there are no graves to recall the exterminated, no cemeteries to recall their ancestors. The town records are gone, probably burned up, just like the files for the year 1887, in which one could probably have found the date of Leah's birth and the names of her parents—if they ever existed.

Well, there must have been a girl past her prime, living nearby and often speaking to me, so that her existence concerned me directly for a while. In those days, and much later, women like Leah treated me like a confidant. More often than not, they inspired me to talk, and they listened with an attentiveness that encouraged me and satisfied my vanity.

Leah is probably a blend of several female figures, older girls, left on the shelf, feeling humiliated anew every day. My sensitivity to their fate was aroused at a very early age, and I am still not free of it. In all my novels, there are characters connected with this real and imaginary Leah.

It was the premature start of spring in the year 1914. Perhaps the horrors that were to burst upon us in August make that spring seem, in retrospect, the happiest time of my life.

Aside from the Pentateuch, which was read through annually, and the prophets Isaiah, Jeremiah, and Amos, who made a deep impact on me that probably still lingers—aside from these great texts and their commentaries, I also read the biblical chronicles. These books not only interested me but also aroused my excitement and indignation at many things and many people—for instance, King David, although we were supposed to honor him as the poet of the psalms. Contrary to the instruction of my tutor and to Jewish tradition, I inferred that uncontrolled men ruled nations, thereby nearly always making bad history. I disliked almost all heroes, except for Samuel and Samson, who was somewhat primitive but full of character, and I was disappointed by Homer's heroes a few short years later. I also discovered the unique and unabating spell of the printed word. I loved German fairy tales—and, even more, Andersen's—and still enjoy reading them today. During that same period I came upon the Nat Pinkerton paperbacks, detective pulp that was all the rage. I read everything I could get my hands on.

In those years, the many volumes of Sholem Aleichem's complete works were coming out. The postman, who brought them to our home, would always notify my father's friends the same day, and they would gather in our house that evening to read the best pieces aloud—mostly monologues, short stories, and comical scenes. They would remain until late at night; just as the writer wished, they all "laughed with one eye and wept with the other." I didn't start reading Yiddish until much later; so for several years, Sholem Aleichem and the two other classical writers of Yiddish literature, Mendele Mokher-Sforim and Yitsik-Leyb Peretz, were authors whose writings I knew without reading them myself. Naturally, the nine-year-old was not able to grasp everything these three so different authors had to say, or to understand them as they meant to be understood.

Sholem Aleichem always made me laugh—less through descriptions of funny situations and ludicrous actions than through the diction of his heroes, who usually delivered monologues in a verbal torrent that couldn't be stemmed. To be sure, they couldn't surprise a Zablotów Jew, for they spoke like the people of the shtetl—and yet quite differently, for the author gave each character some kind of linguistic peculiarity that always exposed the speaker's essence. The special tone lent even the most mundane words unexpected significance, letting the laughers sense early enough that eventually, they would not understand the merriment elicited by this flood of words. Although neither my father nor his friends read well out loud, Sholem Aleichem's art of using individual music to delineate each character had such a powerful effect on me that he more than anyone else made me, as a reader and author, sensitive, even hypersensitive, to all linguistic music.

I distinctly remember that everything seemed more beautiful to me that spring than ever before: the flowers and the trees, the blue of the sky, the green of the meadows along the river. Life itself, which sometimes struck me, like all children, as hard, seemed easier, cheerier. All at once I was certain that the hills would recede and reveal the mountains behind them. The world became larger, vaster; it surrendered to my eyes.

What I was taught in the Polish school could not capture this; it was too simple and was presented in a language that I didn't like and didn't want to learn. However, I did think a great deal about the things my tutor taught me and the things that bombarded me day in and day out, the things I heard at home in the evening, for instance, whenever they read aloud from the green-black-and-red jubilee edition of Sholem Aleichem. All these things were new—they were just what I needed.

Naturally, those wonderful months also had hours of grief and melancholy—the burdens of a child's life, which adults so utterly misinterpret or underestimate. This blend of happiness and misery astounds me even today. I was a truly intelligent child; in everything I encountered, I tried swiftly and clearly to distinguish the essential from the inessential, the indispensable from the casual and incidental. But this never prevented me, if my sensitivity was offended, from reacting foolishly, unjustly, aggressively, or by becoming depressed and withdrawn. Subsequently, as an adult, I came upon the same intermittent stupidity, darkness in broad daylight, the desert in the middle of the oasis. But I will discuss this later.

Perhaps those last months of peace seemed far happier than they really were. Nevertheless, I felt that a new era was dawning for me. This feeling has recurred only a few times in my life, most strongly during my Berlin years, between 1928 and 1933. Something you have barely begun to expect actually takes place; no obstacle appears in your path; every significant action occurs exactly at the right moment; everything is yours for the asking.

Having just completed this sentence, I feel some doubt about it. What really happened in that spring and early summer of 1914, offering so much to a boy in his ninth year of life? What expectation of his was surprisingly fulfilled, just what, exactly, was his for the asking? I am perplexed, for I have no answer. I do recall something I experienced and then described in a still unpublished novel; but it strikes me as quite unlikely that this episode took place in 1914. It was during the summer vacation I spent with my father in Jaremcze, a fashionable Carpathian resort. Yet in July 1914, everything was overshadowed by the disaster that would be triggered at Sarajevo by the assassination of the pretender to the throne. People knew that no one could escape its effects, so I cannot rule it out; but it is highly unlikely that we went on vacation at that time. The episode probably took place in summer 1913—my memory of it must have been off by a year, perhaps because that event would dovetail in more than one respect with the "season of my life" that began some twelve months later.

It was my first encounter with the theater. On a lovely summer evening, my father and I were sitting in a garden restaurant, very close to the platform on which an itinerant troupe of Yiddish actors was going to appear.

The curtain was finally raised, not without problems and various mishaps—which produced the first laughs the players got that evening. The scene was a square in front of an inn. Many years later, I discovered that a butchered version of Goldoni's *The Servant of Two Masters* was what they were performing—that is, would have performed, if they had ever gotten beyond the first act. Initially, everything was marvelous. Truffaldino, that jack-of-all-trades, was everywhere at once. He, who lied so charmingly, was more believable than those who drily told the truth. Whenever he vanished, I waited for him to reappear, wearing his green trousers and little red jacket, and with blue-black curls above his laughing eyes and rosy cheeks.

Suddenly, at the end of the second act, uniformed men strode in, stationing themselves between us and the stage. Their leader interrupted

Truffaldino, shouting, "The show is prohibited! In the name of the law, I hereby arrest the entire troupe for stating false facts, for vagabondage, and for failing to pay their bills!"

Truffaldino replied, "We'll pay our debts to the innkeeper. Try and understand. We're not criminals, we're just unfortunate artists."

But all the policemen were already on stage. The sergeant grabbed Truffaldino and, perhaps out of clumsiness, yanked off his wig, suddenly exposing Truffaldino's bald skull. The child did not know there was such a thing as wigs, and at first he thought the policeman had pulled out the black curls. The child felt immense pain, as though that terrible thing had happened to his own hair. The moment of deepest humiliation, however, came when Truffaldino took off his red jacket, turned it inside-out—it was a shabby brown coat—and then let down his green trousers. Oh, how ugly he was! How old he looked! Nothing remained of his beauty but the red color on his cheeks; yet this too was soon washed away by the old man's tears, shed in rage and embarrassment.

In the decades that have passed since that disrupted, bewildering theatrical evening, the memory of that incident has surfaced infrequently but always with the magnified clarity of a movie close-up. It is not hard to determine what kind of impact this peculiar incident had on me then, and why the memory has persisted. The reader of these memoirs may have already noticed that many of the experiences depicted here involve a sudden shock, the revelation and destruction of an "as if," a dramatic disillusionment. Nothing, nobody is really transformed, no black or white magic is at work. Truffaldino was not changed into a poor, ugly, old man. He was merely stripped of illusion and degraded by being made to appear as he really was.

This experience would have been more meaningful at a subsequent period of my life—one year later, when I was "learning" the biblical books of Judges, Chronicles, and Samuel. I liked young David, of course, but only now did I discover that he had sent a man, who had served him loyally, to his death in order to get his wife. As I have already mentioned, I became profoundly distrustful of heroes. Every one of them acted as if his beginning were already his completion, but the higher he ascended, the more certain it became for him who wanted to see that almost everything was illusion: a komedye, as the children in the shtetl yelled whenever they saw through a sham.

Only a few more pages, and I will take leave of my shtetl—or rather my pre-World War I childhood. How much will remain unsaid! I am most strongly oppressed by the feeling that I have once again written a fragment. So many images surface, events and experiences offer themselves to my memory, virtually a goodbye, a last farewell. For I am dealing here not just with my early years, but with something that goes far beyond biography: I am dealing with the murdered shtetl, with a religious, social, and communal entity, a community of which I am one of the last survivors.

Urtshy was a tall old man who held himself as straight as a birch tree. In my memory, everything about him is white—which may explain the comparison with a birch tree. Not only his long beard and his sidelocks and his shaven head, but also his shirt, which he wore without a tie, and his long socks—everything was white. Furthermore, he was well known for wearing a white smock on holidays instead of the black gaberdine. It was his professional costume, which made him known throughout the villages where he always worked as a cantor. His fee was usually paid in kind: food and kegs of moonshine, which the Jews (and their Gentile neighbors) distilled legally, but more often secretly.

Urtshy was the first drinker I ever met. He and my grandfather had been fellow "learners" in their youth and remained close friends for the rest of their lives. The two of them might show up at any time, even very late at night, asking for my father, with whom Urtshy always had something "very important" to discuss. But it was usually just a pretext to wet his whistle—for which he needed at least two shots of liquor. He almost never accepted an invitation to a meal, claiming that his son was expecting him. But everyone knew that his daughter-in-law didn't like having him over and seldom allowed him across her threshold.

Like my great-grandfather Borekh, Urtshy, impelled by a foreboding, would sometimes leave home, walking over to the bridge or climbing the hill behind the river in order to welcome the approaching Messiah. But he usually came back early enough to go to a synagogue and help observe a *yortseit*, the anniversary of a death, which meant getting his share of the liquor contributed by every close relative of the deceased. If no such benefactor was present, then Urtshy or one of his boon companions would recall that this was the yortsait of some great scholar, rabbi, or preacher, and he wouldn't relent until the worshipers donated a few crowns for a liter of moonshine and poppy cakes. This old man had something domineering about him, which didn't so much intimidate people as make them wish to please him.

Why do I now think of a man whom I probably knew little more than that he had been widowed early on, that he was a drinker and also one of my grandfather's best friends? Because of an odd incident, which took place on the last major autumn holiday. It was Simchas-Torah, the festival of rejoicing in the Torah (each year the Jews thank God anew for charging them with carrying his laws). Late that night, someone knocked at our door, first hesitantly, then more and more vehemently. I awoke and listened. My father let in a man and switched on the light in his study. I got up, partly out of curiosity, but also to make sure my father wasn't in any danger. Through the glass window I saw Urtshy; once again all in white, he sat upright on the couch, his head lolling back and forth.

"I can't sleep," he said, without opening his eyes.

"Why?" asked my father.

"Something awful has happened. I forgot the words of the night prayer—I've said it every night of my life, and now suddenly it's gone—forgotten! Recite it for me, but very slowly. I'm not as sober as I ought to be."

And I heard my father, who stood before him, slowly recite the great night prayer—not the short one for children—word for word. Urtshy repeated it with great effort; if he mispronounced a word, he would correct himself until it finally came out right. But no sooner had he spoken the final *amen* than he collapsed, dead to the world. My father covered him up.

How far away that all is now. But as far away as I have come from those worshipers, from the worshipers of all religions, I still find it hard not to feel deep emotion whenever I recall Urtshy, who would not let sleep overpower him until he spoke the final word of the long night prayer. He was not acting from fear of angering God through an omission; rather, he was driven by that peculiar Hasidic love for God, who is the worshiper's giving, serving older brother and comforter. Since the shtetl was occupied by enemies and finally destroyed, the Urtshys have taken on a significance for me that I would never have previously attributed to them; they remain alive in me, as they had never been previously. I do not recall ever trying to find out what became of Urtshy, for instance, whether he even survived World War I and whether he stayed on in Zablotow after that. We never returned after our final escape; and just two years later, I lost interest in the shtetl and its inhabitants, even the Urtshys and Leahs. I am reluctant to write the sentence that urges itself upon me: Vienna devoured me. But the word "devoured" seems wrong somehow—it exaggerates an exaggeration.

PART TWO

War and Flight

Perhaps the memory is skewed despite its clarity. It was a Friday evening; the heat of the day wouldn't let up. We had not yet completed the Sabbath dinner when we heard the loud blare of a trumpet. The sound came from the marketplace, down the large street, toward our house. Who dared to do that on the eve of the Sabbath? What did it mean?

A neighbor burst into the room; she said Max was blowing the trumpet to put everyone on the alert. Why? What had happened? It was war, the young woman answered in agitation, as though reeling between pleasure at the sensational news and fear that her husband, who was visiting his parents in the countryside, would be called up and—God forbid!—be placed in danger. Well, for now, there was only a general mobilization, Max explained, suddenly standing at the table with the trumpet under his arm. Looking at him, you would have thought he had announced that the Messiah had come. His eyes were different that night—not piercing or searching, but joyful. And the laughter accompanying his words wasn't malicious or gleeful, but happy.

"It's a disaster," said my father, and turned away from Max, who, disappointed by this reception, strode over to the door and replied, "Why a disaster? The kaiser will win; the czar will be beaten so badly that he will never again dare to oppress a single one of his subjects."

"For us, every war is a disaster," said my father. "No one knows who of us in this room will live to see the peace."

"I have to report for military duty the day after tomorrow," said

Max, "and I'm not scared. It'll all be over in a couple of weeks, and I'll come back as a platoon leader, maybe even a sergeant. In a battle, no one asks who your father is."

Having said these words, Max left us. We promptly heard the blare again, but soon we stopped thinking about the trumpet and the future sergeant. A lot of voices became audible, mostly female; young and old women, more joining them on the way, were going to the cemetery on the hill. They prayed and wept at the graves of their ancestors, whose weathered headstones were half-devoured by the earth. The mourners begged the dead for help, asking them to intercede with the Almighty. I had never seen anything like it. Although I understood the expression "consulting the dead," the loud wailing of these women at the nocturnal graves was so eerie—as if something completely alien, something more dangerous than any intangible or physical threat, had suddenly invaded our lives.

The next day, the eeriness was replaced by a strange, festive excitement. Young men were going off to war; they were brought to the train by their parents or wives, who did not conceal their fear of the future. Although muffled sobs could be heard the whole time, there was a mood of expectation, a mood more hopeful than anxious. There wouldn't be a real war, people were saying, and it certainly wouldn't last for more than a few weeks. The kaiser in Vienna knew what he was doing, everyone was saying. He wanted to teach the czar a lesson, so that he could never again try to attack Austria. *Fonye**—that is, the czar—was responsible for all evil. During the cold season, whenever violent easterly and northeasterly winds whipped up, almost tearing the houses out of the ground, even the children knew what this meant: the czar was hanging innocent people in his empire. And many songs sung in every Jewish home deplored Russia. One was a lullaby whose words have not yet faded from my mind:

> Only the wind brings you greetings
> From the distant land:
> From Siberia, your father
> Sends you greetings, my child.
>
> There he stands, shovel in hand,
> Digging deeper, ever deeper,

*[Trans. note: Yiddish for "Russian."]

Tearing up the cold, hard earth,
Digging a grave for the enemy, the czar.

After every pogrom, Jews came across the border. They stayed for a while, then went on, heading for a port so they could leave Europe forever. They might have a husband or son in America; work was waiting for them there. Directly or circuitously, they traveled as far west as possible, away from Fonye's Russia. Often women with infants would appear in the marketplace: the ones whose songs moved the donors were given the most:

Jews, sons of charitable people,
Help, give,
Give winding-cloths for the dead,
With the living share your bread.

Since the Dreyfus Affair and the Pogrom of Kishinev, nothing had impressed and excited the Zablotow Jews as much as the ritual-murder trial of Beilis. Now, when the war broke out, they could at first conceal their fear and disgust only by thinking of the enemy, the czar, whose downfall they had been dreaming of for decades. They were quite confident that the victory of the Austro-Hungarian empire would bring about a just and democratic regime in Russia and thereby the emancipation of her Jews.

During the first few weeks of the war, the mood in the shtetl was virtually manic-depressive; optimism rapidly alternated with fear of a Russian invasion, pogroms, famine, and epidemics. In the same breath people spoke of miracles that would be worked by technology or by some wonder rabbi, very soon, or at least before it was too late. If thunder boomed far away, people wondered whether it was cannon or an approaching storm. Minds were quickly put at ease, for it was certain that Austria had the best artillery in the world, and that her border was so skillfully protected the enemy would assault the fortifications in vain and bleed to death in these useless attacks. Neither in this remote corner of the monarchy nor elsewhere could anyone have guessed that although a certain Lieutenant Redl, the head of an Austria military secret service, had already sold all plans to the Russians, the Austrians did not change a single tactical or strategic detail after the betrayal was exposed. People were surprised when the Russians effortlessly took the famous Fort

Halycz. During its retreat, the Austro-Hungarian army avenged Redl's betrayal by hanging Ruthenian priests and village teachers for suspected but unproved espionage.

Early one morning, we left Zablotow as if we were going on a long summer vacation in the country. We knew the Russians might advance all the way to the Prut and occupy our shtetl—not for long, of course, people said. But we wanted to avoid even one day of Russian occupation. Tracz, the hamlet where we were planning to spend some time, was probably the most out-of-the-way spot in Galicia, truly the back of beyond. It was also one of the poorest areas, and its meager population was retrograde in every respect. Tracz too had a "manor"—which was what we called (usually inaccurately) every large farm belonging to a Polish nobleman or city-dweller. A "manor" normally included a single large house, which contrasted majestically with the thatched huts scattered widely through the countryside. My father brought us here because he believed no troops would ever turn up in this area; the route leading here was certainly not marked on any map, if only because there was no real road. Furthermore, Tracz lay amid densely forested hills, which covered it so thoroughly that only a fluke could bring a mounted patrol here.

I seem to recall an especially beautiful autumn. Together with the children of the tenant farmer and those of the peasants who worked for him, we formed a small gang of boys and girls. We were happy because there was no school, and we thought there would be none for a long time.

I often break off as I write because I feel drawn to my balcony, where one can see the Eiffel Tower on the right side of the horizon and, much closer, high and low rooftops, the glass domes and glass walls of artists' studios, which are especially numerous in this district. Here, a few steps from Boulevard Montparnasse, in the heart of the Left Bank of Paris, I am at home, as I was in Vienna, and then, until 1933, in Berlin; yet not in the same way as in the tiny shtetl of my childhood and in an altogether different way from how I felt in Tracz, the remote nest where we sought refuge from the war. When I think back to those early months of World War I, I feel as if I had gazed with the same insatiable eyes at the huts between the fields, which sloped up to the edge of the forest. Dust whirls up and the noise of a wagon recedes, its wheels creaking so lamentably that you imagine you're hearing the stubborn moans of old people. That was how I, standing at the gate, stared out into the world, listening to every sound—I looked forward to a change in the peaceful, uneventful mood, and yet I just as greatly feared a change. Beyond the vast forest everything was in constant motion, for something was happening there, something important and dangerous, from which we had fled.

Yes, we were lucky to be so far away from the shooting, and, I often heard it said, we should thank God every day, for we were safely ensconced in a secret corner, as on a hidden island in the dead arm of a raging river. We children were happy, especially during the day, even when the rains finally came, driving us indoors, where we had to *"learn"* again. But whenever I was alone or woke up at night, I was torn by an inner conflict. It was good and sensible to be in Tracz, but we were lost here because we weren't where grand events followed one another so swiftly that no moment was like the next. One evening, my father said, "If the war doesn't end soon, we'd be better off giving up our hiding-place and going to Vienna. The good schools there remain open even during the war, so the children won't lose time, no matter how long we have to wait for peace. Our wagon has sound springs, and our horses are strong and well fed. We could make our way to Hungary circuitously, along side roads, and then take the train to Vienna."

No sooner had I heard this plan than I began to picture the initially difficult trip through the mountains—all the hazards and our dealing with them, and finally our arrival in Vienna. One and a half years later, everything came about exactly as the nine-year-old had imagined it in great detail. Without ever putting it into words, I believed (as I later believed) in the power of wishes that strive to come true so long as you persist and keep hoping. But for the moment, the obstacles seemed so great; furthermore, people hoped that after its initial victories in Galicia, the Russian army would suffer a crucial defeat, as in Tannenberg, and the czar would quickly surrender. Also, my parents were afraid of being in a foreign place, where they would be only refugees and would soon become poor. We would have to remain near our own people and do everything possible to protect our property. I didn't like these arguments, for they blocked our road to Vienna.

In that utterly remote, out-of-the-way corner of the monarchy, *Wien*, the monosyllabic name of the capital and residency, always had an inspiring effect. It was not only a nine-year-old boy for whom Vienna meant splendor and glory, absolute beauty on earth, the city of palaces that were built not of brick and stone, but of radiant crystal, on which the night never dared to fall. Many like me dreamed of some day living in the imperial city and, like the native Viennese, admiring Franz Joseph I daily in his marvelous carriage, which was drawn by white horses. I loved to picture the kaiser inviting me together with other Jewish boys to a dinner in his castle. How were we to behave? How should we deal with the problem that the food was certainly not kosher, since the monarch was Catholic, but that at the same time, we mustn't offend our host? Aside from this obstacle, such a visit seemed very tempting. We would sing him our songs and provide highly intelligent answers to even the most difficult questions that he and his advisers would ask us; but we would be restrained, so that they wouldn't think we were showing off. And I even prepared the words to describe this great event to my family afterward. Emperor Franz Joseph I meant far more to all the shtetl Jews throughout the monarchy than to any other subjects, for the Jews viewed him as the guarantor of their civil rights, their protector against hatred and despotism.

Whenever I read the Viennese newspaper aloud to my grandfather (about two or three times a week), he wanted to hear first everything written about the kaiser, and only then the news from around the world, especially the reports on the Balkan wars, which followed one another in rapid succession. I didn't know why he was so interested in the "paralyzed Turk" (the nickname for the Ottoman Empire). I myself focused on the tangle of main and relative clauses, which, I was told, proved that the editors of *Die Neue Freie Presse* wrote marvelous German. No wonder— since everything that came from Vienna had to be marvelous. Nor was Leah the only one who thought so. In the shtetl she had given me detailed descriptions of the life I would someday lead in Vienna. Though she would be an old woman, perhaps forty, she would not shrink from the trip; she would visit me, and we would go driving along the Praterallee in a carriage with rubber wheels.

I kept yearning for the big city until that July 27, 1916, when, after a long stay in a provisional refugee camp in Moravia, we reached Vienna by way of Brno. My yearning was like a child's homesickness, which is certainly one of the most oppressive emotions. At the same time, I felt almost like a traitor leaving Tracz, which was a village in name only. For one thing, I feared losing something in this dead corner: the feeling of safety and security, which makes a child or an adult feel in harmony with his condition and with himself. There was something else, too, though I do not now exactly what it was.

I have never felt homesick for Zablotow, which I have not seen since 1916 and will never see again. But I did feel nostalgia for the last house in the last village during my youth in Vienna; it has haunted me all my life. No, I have never daydreamed about being a happy tiller of the soil, plowing, sowing, reaping. Rather, I pictured myself as outside the hustle and bustle, listening in deep silence and seldom hearing anything but the throbbing of my own heart, sometimes the soughing of the wind or the warning shrieks of crows. Listening and motionlessly gazing around, fearing nothing and expecting nothing. There was a variant of this image, which frequently recurred: women in Ukrainian costumes, trudging back from the fields, suddenly turning into the empty village street. Their trudging seems to make the air move. A single, strong voice sounds out, soon the others take up the melody, then they fall silent, and the first voice begins again. Whenever I hear a record of Ukrainian peasant women, their singing affects me even more strongly than the melodies of our prayers or of Hasidic songs in bringing my childhood so close that the irretrievable past seems directly adjacent to the present, as if there were still a road leading to it.

Granted, I was happy when we went home again after a few months. The countryside was covered with snow, the horses often lost the invisible roads, the sleighs glided silently over the high snow, plunged into ditches and had to be arduously hauled out again. I thought I would forget Tracz quickly, for we had gotten fed up with it during the past few weeks. Cossack patrols had turned up on the outskirts of the forests; the horsemen, armed with rifles, sabers, and lances, remained for only a few minutes. We heard they had asked an old lame man where the Orthodox priest was. When they learned there was none in this village, they supposedly beat the old man, threatening to sleep with his mother. People suspected that they had lost their way en route to a village near a country road which was only three leagues from the imperial highway.

Be that as it may, my parents now felt that Tracz was no longer safe; indeed, it might easily become more dangerous than our shtetl, which had already been occupied for weeks.

I experienced a number of things for the first time in that tiny village, good things and bad. Although few were important or pertinent, many of them have remained in my memory. Only one first experience, which was to remain ever present, has recurred a number of times in different circumstances. It was right after the first snowfall. My father was traveling by sleigh to a relatively out-of-the-way small town, which supposedly had escaped enemy occupation. He wanted to purchase various household items and also obtain supplies for the winter. He took the large sleigh and the best horses. One of the farmhands went along, a grumpy, elderly man, who was familiar with the entire countryside and could supposedly find his way even if the roads were invisible under the snow. On that day, the dark-gray sky hung down deep, but no snow fell. The brightness came from the white earth, not from above. The evening set in unexpectedly; the ground shone very dimly. I knew that only the neighing of the horses would herald the approach of the travelers, for the sleigh had no bells, which could have attracted a patrol.

I kept peering through the window, more and more expectant and confident as the first few hours wore by. Now it was eight o'clock—now nine: It could only be a few more minutes. I didn't want to eat or drink, but then I had to go to bed with the other children. I remained awake, listening, hearing the adults talking. Their voices were too soft, I couldn't understand what they said. Soon the shimmer of light under the door vanished; the house, swathed in darkness and silence, became eerie, for it seemed not to be awaiting my father's return, as though my mother and our hosts were not worried about him. At this late hour, he could be wandering through the gigantic forest, unable to find the road—or else Silko, the farmhand, had gotten liquored up in the town, and now the horses and the sleigh and my father and the drunkard were lying in some chasm, seriously injured. Or they had been surprised by Cossacks and were now their prisoners, being tortured so they would reveal the location of the farm where we were hiding from the Russians. Or else the Cossacks had found their tracks and then waited for the loaded sleigh to come back from the town. They had shot my father and beaten Silko bloody before letting him go. He would certainly freeze to death before anyone found him. And the Cossacks were divvying up the loot. Or else they were bandits, who always ambushed wayfarers on long winter nights, when they had enough time to wipe out any trail and reach safety with their loot.

I saw all these things as if they were taking place before my eyes. I was kept awake not by fear but by the overwhelming certainty that we were helpless in the face of evil, no matter what guise it assumed. The balance of power had shifted so thoroughly that my father was now as defenseless as the poorest, weakest, stupidest shtetl inhabitant could ever have been. It was only during the subsequent days that I tried to fathom what had happened to God and his omnipotence in a world so deeply altered. Yet, during that long sleepless night, I did not think of him or his help. Nor did I think that I might at any moment become one of those orphan boys who had to praise the name of God several times a day with the kaddish prayer. All night long, I was at the mercy of my imagination, which showed me possibilities, horrors, but also comforts, the rescue of my father, his attempt to defend himself, to flee the enemy or strike him down and, right after that, his bloody face or lifeless body, stripped of his heavy fur coat and his jacket, in the snow next to the capsized sleigh.

The tormenting anxiety that drove away my sleep made me worry about a person I loved, but it did not perplex me. In the course of that night, all my images of what might have happened to him became as real as if they were precise memories of true experiences. During those hours, I learned—no, mastered—the meaning of fear: a demystified, realistic fear.

I fell asleep just before daybreak. I was awakened by my father, who had returned around noon. He had not left the town until morning, because it would have been too dangerous to travel at night. Silko was so drunk he would never have been able to find the way.

I was dumbstruck at seeing my father standing so close, at my bedside, uninjured, smiling, as if nothing had happened that night. No one noticed my surprise; everyone was talking at once. I never told anybody about the fictitious adventures of that night, but I am always anxious about the delay of visitor or a message. And during every such delay, I am mute, unable to communicate with the people around me, as I envision those imaginary catastrophes. Had I told my mother how worried I was about my father that night, she could certainly have calmed my fears, probably assuring me that he would obviously stay away all night if he didn't finish his errands on time. Yet whenever this special fear has plagued me since then, it has always thrown me back on my own resources, as if it were a secret I should keep because the life of the person I am worried about depends on it.

We had spent only a few months in Tracz; for us children, it was an extended vacation. And compared with what we would go through soon after coming home, the days in Tracz were empty and uneventful. Yet as I think back to that far-flung spot while writing, I realize that it has assumed unusual importance in my "disactualized" memory without my being fully aware of it. Whenever I have sought comfort by daydreaming about a quiet, perfectly happy life "in the remotest village," I have—if somewhat dimly—recalled Tracz.

Whenever someone I care for is inexplicably late, I get all sorts of terrifying images—and I think of Tracz. When I was forty, I composed a plot that begins in a village; the hero, a native of that village, circuitously reaches a field not far from Vienna, where he bleeds to death from a wound. I was obviously writing under the influence of the picture of Tracz as it had stamped itself on my mind when I was nine years old. The hero's widow says:

> The houses in our village are huts, the walls and floors are clay, the roofs are thatched. . . . We have seasons too, but our countryside belongs to the fall, with every season the fall secretly returns. . . . The crows nest everywhere in our village. In their croaking, the autumn speaks even on days when the land might forget it. . . . Yet nowhere in the world do people sing as much as in our village. The crows fall silent only when we sing. . . . In those summer days, when the war was still so young that it was no more unlike a vague promise than a threat—that was the first time that the village seemed forgotten by the fall. The rains failed to come for a long time, the blue of the sky seemed permanent.

It was an extremely cold day when we left the village in two open sleighs. The smoke was meandering from the chimneys of the larger huts; the smaller ones looked like distant gray tarpaulins spread out on the snow. Neither man nor beast was to be seen; only a dog barked in long, drawn-out bursts; its howling accompanied us until we were over the hill.

A few hours later, in the afternoon, it finally happened: Russian soldiers stopped us at the bridge leading across the Prut to our shtetl. My father was taken to the customs booth to show his papers and to explain where we were coming from and where we were going. One of the soldiers, a big man with shiny blue eyes, leaned over to my mother and asked her where our home was. She hesitated for an instant, then gave him false information. He laughed contentedly, my mother blushed. At thirty-six, she was no longer considered young in those days, but she was still a beautiful, certainly desirable woman. I observed the scene very closely and, I think, understood it perfectly. I felt she was right to give the soldier the wrong address; but I was confused by the fact that she then blushed so deeply. They soon allowed us across the bridge, and a few minutes later we were home. Like the others, who had remained in the shtetl, we would have to get used to the Russian occupation and make it through the bad time until peace, which had to be imminent.

Sometimes when I watch television in the evening and learn about the day's events through words and images, I am astonished that time can apparently be cut into thin slices like bread. I say "apparently," for nothing resists fragmentation so violently as time in its inexorable flow. However, we experience it in a continuously changing articulation, sometimes broadly, as it were, sometimes as a sequence of tiny points, rapidly uniting into a line or, vice versa, expanding inordinately, so that a tiny section becomes a long, unending stretch. It is as if a carefree ignoramus were adding or multiplying fractions without first reducing them to a common denominator. One reason the experience of time does not become chaotic in memory is that the person remains the unchangeable, unshakable center; acting as a dam and sluice, he continually regulates or thinks he regulates the flow of time.

"You ought to know that the only precision I absolutely value is that of a clock. I have renounced any other." These words are spoken in a critical situation by one of my characters, a Polish count named Skarbek, who is a passionate gambler. I invented him with genuine if ironic sympathy. He tends to remain ambiguous but can be quite trustworthy as long as gambling or love affairs do not take his mind off what he really ought to be doing. He believes traditionally in the God of the Catholic Church; he has faith and hope that the boundlessly gracious Mother of God will eventually intervene. But in his daily life, he believes only in the clock.

I think that I too have been obsessed with time since my early youth, more precisely since the early, abrupt, cruel end of my childhood in winter 1915. What I began to feel then was something I kept expressing over and over again much later—the last time was in 1959, forty-four years later, in my book on Alfred Adler:

> Our relationship to time is determined by the fact that we are in time only to the extent that it penetrates us. . . . Time articulates our conscious being. In it we are like a swimmer who can never leave the water; that is one reason why he is sure to drown in it some day; we consume time and are consumed by it until it ultimately devours us.

An inner world like the one my childhood was shaped by, so obsessively tied to an old, virtually encyclopedic tradition, grants far more room to the past than to the present. It even justifies hope for the future with the promises and predictions of a past whose burden everyone must regard as an asset if not a privilege. The present thus becomes nothing but a passageway, both an epilogue and prologue, yet tiny in itself—enormously important at the moment, but simply for the moment. This is not why we were born, this is not the goal of our lives; our true goal is "the coming world," that is, eternity. The present? It is not a bridge of iron and not a Messianic bridge of cigarette paper, for no sooner had you crossed it than it dissolved into nothingness. Always looking for the hills beyond the hills, I lived in anticipation of the "time beyond time."

Soon after our return to the shtetl, everything changed, at first only in part, but a few weeks later completely. Certain things happened and, as a result, every day, every hour, stretched out so immeasurably that, figuratively speaking, the first hill suddenly appeared to swallow all the hills beyond it. Forget nothing that has happened and always think of what will be some day—this demand remained; but the morning that was just dawning, the night that wore on as if it would never end, over-shadowed all past and all future. Bursting with events, the moment swelled up, becoming huge, threatening to remain everlasting, like a pain that turns life into suffering.

The shtetl was cut off from the outside world. Mail was stopped to and from the unoccupied portion of the monarchy, and the shtetl seldom received a sign of life even from neutral countries. So many families had depended on the few dollars that came with letters from their relatives in America, who usually promised to send steamship tickets and looked forward to welcoming them in New York. But now, no letters or dollars arrived; poverty became an oppressive hardship from which there was no escape. The occupation troops confiscated the food, so prices rose daily. There was not enough bread for the poor, too little coal in that icy winter, barely any wood even though the forests were so near. If you wanted to leave the precincts of the shtetl, you needed a pass, which you could obtain only by applying for one and bribing the sergeant.

The shtetl starved and froze. Not everyone, but nearly everyone: only the poor; yet they had always been the majority, and now they were poorer than ever. That was why so many of them fell ill: first the children, then the old people, then so many others. And one day, each person whispered it to the next: In this house or that, a few people were terribly sick. Dangerously, they said, dangerous not only for their own families, but for all the inhabitants. Next, we could read it in an announcement on yellow paper put up by the military command; partly calligraphic, partly scrawled, it said: "Cases of typhoid fever have been positively identified by the battalion medical unit. To prevent any spread of the disease, this township is to be isolated from the outside world, effective immediately. All still valid passes are hereby declared invalid. No outsider may enter the township, no inhabitant thereof may leave it." These sentences were followed by threats and hygiene instructions, which were described as strict orders. For instance, the severest penalties were imposed on any family that failed to place a visible sign at the entrance to its home if any person living in the household fell ill. The houses of prayer and study as well as the schools were to shut down until further notice. Any assembly of civilians, except for funerals, was strictly prohibited.

The closing of the schools and houses of prayer struck the townsfolk much harder than the belated announcement that an epidemic had broken out. Some people claimed the typhoid would not spread; the cold would virtually freeze it. "So," they concluded, "all these measures aren't worth a pinch of snuff. Prohibiting us from going to the house of prayer, forcing us to make our children degenerate in the darkness of ignorance—only a servant of the czar would come up with anything like that."

More people than usual came to evening prayers, and the children were sent to heder; they were urged to *learn* harder than ever, memorize every word of the Bible—because this epidemic was most certainly a well-deserved punishment.

The nights of an elderly man are usually fragmented. Granted, he is far more seldom roused—actually driven—from sleep by dramatic or melodramatic dreams. On the other hand, he drowses far more frequently especially just before dawn. He then has to wake up before he can fall asleep again with some effort. He virtually wanders through hypnagogic states and half-dreams as he hovers between sleeping and waking. In his regained slumber, he sometimes has an odd sense of frail happiness, to which he clings as if his life depended on it.

Only the person who has been a prisoner without hope, who has lived in the crushing loneliness of solitary confinement, knows that sleep is a lifesaving haven, from which one can return to the past of the pariah, strengthened, in new armor. And it was in solitary confinement that I became tensely awake, immediately, with no transition, no matter who awakened me. My mind and my senses were as keen and attentive as if they hadn't returned from that distant place, that haven that separated you from the misery of being imprisoned by the enemy, from the fear of the coming day. Before going to sleep, I would pick a special topic that I wanted to think about, without losing a moment, as soon as I awoke. It could even be a song of many stanzas, which I intended to sing to myself very faintly, or a poem, which I would recite very softly. This was a psychological trick to protect myself against the depression of early morning.

At present, I have no trick. I never shield myself against invading thoughts and feelings, which are sometimes as unwelcome as frost in spring. But now that I am writing this book, these intruders most often involve my childhood, or what I have written during the last few days, or, less often, what I will or should write.

Today, when I woke up with a start, the epidemic came to me not as a memory but as a word, then as a mood, which was certainly dominated by fear, perhaps terror, yet linked to an overstimulated curiosity.

Back then, we learned on the same day that there were no new cases, but that the typhoid epidemic was spreading rapidly; that this disease was not fatal, it couldn't have caused the deaths. In the same breath, people said that the victims were dying like flies. The rumors followed one another nonstop; they fed both hope and despair equally. I find that mood this morning again as well as the (oddly enough) not unpleasant confusion forced on almost everyone by the extreme swings of the pendulum.

What does all that mean to me now? A memory of events, of experiences? Or a *memory of memories*, which have recurred in the course of half a century, faded, "disactualized," coming whenever one of the characteristic disasters of our era has threatened our existence?

The light peeping through the cracks of the curtains remains gray for a long time, then turns white and gradually golden. The discreet pealing of bells at the monastery that was turned into a boarding school will probably not awaken any other sleeper; they once again remind me of how beneficial the silence filling my bedroom is, so that, in the middle of the big city, I live as if I were in the last house of that out-of-the-way village in Savoy, which for many long years, was a second, better Tracz for me.

During that typhoid epidemic, which was not so much replaced as accompanied by a smallpox epidemic, I was often awakened by loud weeping. The victims seemed to die more frequently toward the end of night than at other times. But this may have been inaccurate: in the nocturnal stillness, you could more clearly hear the cries of the family trying to hold back the dying person, as if he were leaving of his own free will. I can almost hear those words today: "Father, don't abandon us! You're leaving us all alone! We're your children!" I can hear the melody of the lament for the dead, which so often roused me from sleep. I probably opened my eyes, seeking calm in the red shimmer which fell from the screen of the stove to the floor. I didn't have to wonder for long; it was easy to guess who was breathing his last or had just died.

I had already seen two corpses up close: the adolescent stranger with yellow soles whom they had fished from the river, and Jadzia, who had been disguised as a sleeping princess. But the corpses I now had to see every day were different. Their faces were distorted; some lay there as if their terrible cramp had only relaxed that very instant. And their loved ones sobbed as if they had suffered a dreadful injustice, which they deserved much less than other people. Even worse, they now had to worry about the rest of the family and themselves. And that was what sometimes confused me, arousing the as yet unarticulated suspicion that, while the survivors were actually weeping for their dead, sobbing loudly and screaming as if enduring constant torture, they were simultaneously weeping for themselves, fearing for themselves, mourning for themselves most deeply of all.

I yearned for a complete hush and ardently wished that the night would not end for me until I had slept my fill. That was what I desired, but I was also present everywhere: in the homes of other people, whose calls for help could be heard out in the street; in the diminishing crowd that accompanied the dead to the old cemetery on the hill—I was not the only child who, driven by overstimulated curiosity, witnessed events that were strangely exciting and monotonous at once, like any human disaster that occurs on a massive scale and lasts too long.

Other children in Zablotow probably also discovered that during a disaster some people lost all dignity and nearly all their reason, that others became inhumanly ugly, while still others achieved a dignity that made them unreachable. These people fell silent for many hours, whole days; no word seemed to penetrate their solitude. At graves and in the house of prayer, men recited the prayer for the dead; their lips moved tremblingly, but no sound came out.

Did I already know that, although worried about myself and my family, I was already feverishly intent on observing people, their faces, their movements? I don't think so, for since the world we lived in was out of joint, one no longer noticed unusual things.

The occupation commander was convinced that these shtetl Jews were completely insane, because they still sent their children to school despite the danger and the strict prohibition. He therefore set up guards at the houses of study and twice as many at the houses of prayer; he also had the windows of the latter walled up halfway. The Jews then surreptitiously removed the Torah scrolls from the sacred arks and distributed them, to worship in private homes that had been spared by the disease or completely emptied.

I have only spotty recollections of all this. Some things, however, I remember clearly as if my mind had retained a written account of those events instead of a direct memory. For this reason, certain events must have lost the character of immediate experiences, turning into vicarious ones for me. Such modifications are probably caused by an alienation that you wish for at the moment of the event and that comes about immediately or perhaps much later, in retrospect.

Many things could have triggered this process, including something I experienced two or three weeks after the start of the epidemic: a *monotonous sensation,* a kind of egotistical grief, the mourners' fear for themselves. My distrust, my childishly cruel impatience toward the sometimes much too noisy, insistent wailing may also have developed because my own family was untouched by typhoid and smallpox until the very end. We could tell ourselves that we had withstood the ordeal precisely because we had been spared. Had I been older, I would have sympathized more with the wailing women, who wanted to tear out their hair, who threw themselves into the open graves, trying to keep their dead from being lowered into the ground. The louder, the longer a person shrieks out his grief, the less comfort he needs, the less he deserves—I must have discovered this back then. All I can state with any certainty is that I was impressed by a certain style—so that I wanted to become like the people who practiced it so tragically: the style of mute mourners, unaffected dignity, authenticity of existence that rejected all sham. I held aloof from the others after the early weeks of catastrophe; when I had observed them closely, I lived with them in repugnant yet unavoidable intimacy.

However, entirely different events, suffered by all of us, put an early end to my childhood. The frontlines had started shifting; the Austro-Hungarian army left its positions in the Carpathians and was about to drive the Russians across the borders. It was the middle of winter. The men sank knee-deep into the snow, advancing arduously as if they were wading through swamps. In that white world, every living creature looked like a black animal, a raven slowly strutting across the snowy plain.

Despite the epidemic, our shtetl had become a comfortable billet for the Russian occupiers, who hoped to spend the war winter there. But now, Zablotow suddenly became involved in the rapidly expanding sector. The booming of cannon drew closer every day, more and more ominous. The host of wounded men, trudging through the shtetl or carried in straw-covered sleighs, increased daily. There was no field hospital for them, there were no orderlies, no food. They were followed by smashed regiments that were now withdrawing, while reserves marched in to replace them. A retreating unit, an occupation force that senses its days are numbered—nothing is more dangerous for the inhabitants, the civilians, who eye the beaten soldiers with ill-concealed glee as they eagerly wait to cheer the arrival of their own victorious troops as liberators. At first, only the stragglers and marauders came to loot, usually at midnight. Then, when the battle for the bridgehead on the Prut was unavoidable, the occupation troops began to pillage before retreating or advancing to the frontlines. They were already familiar with the area. At first their looting was nonviolent; but then, usually drunk, these soldiers grew violent, smashing their rifle butts into the backs, chests, and finally heads of the victimized inhabitants. There were very few rapes; any such attempts were usually prevented by other people. The drunken soldiers were often intimidated by the cry, "Fear God!" The population hoped that the looters would avoid the homes of the sick, but the soldiers didn't fear contagion. They figured that if they had enough vodka in their stomachs, they'd be immune to typhoid and smallpox.

No, it was not a pogrom, but the probably inevitable accompaniment of a defeat: the unscrupulous action of an occupation unit that had already received its evacuation order or was expecting it at any moment. The older people applied their knowledge, handed down to them for centuries, millennia. It's always been like this, they said, and it'll always be like this, they repeated. It is written: "If the clay pitcher falls on the rock—woe unto the pitcher! And if the rock falls on the pitcher—woe unto the pitcher!" Even the children instantly grasped that we were clay pitchers and the others the rocks—the alien warriors and perhaps even our own people, as we shall see.

On the other hand, the knowledgeable explained, it's a good omen that they're so wild. It means that they themselves realize how little time they've got left. They'll soon retreat, and we'll be rid of them. It was obvious to everyone that the worst evil portended something better, if not altogether good.

So much had changed in the course of a few weeks. What else could happen to us? The nights, which had so often been alarming ever since the epidemic had spread, were no longer the isolated stretches of time in which people find refuge and quiet, a source of new strength. It began one night before dawn. The shtetl was bombarded by the artillery of the advancing Austrians (no doubt, by some error) and then by the Russians. The Austrians wanted to keep the retreat route under fire, the Russians wanted to destroy the enemy's pontoons. All that either side managed to do was wipe out many of the wooden shacks of the poor, set them on fire, and damage a few houses on the main street. When dawn finally came, the cannon could shoot accurately. But by now nearly all the inhabitants were in the basements, which offered some protection even though they weren't very deep. We also heard the rattle of rifles clearly enough. From time to time, some rapid fire bagan. It sounded closer, but then it suddenly stopped. The lull might last for several minutes, perhaps even half an hour. People left their basements and peered about cautiously, looking down toward the river, up toward the graveyard hill, and over to the bridge. There wasn't much to see. In any case, the Austrians weren't there yet, and all we could see of the Russians was a small patrol, running about, popping up here and there. The short day wore on but seemed longer than the longest summer day. Supposedly, a few people who had ventured out had been killed, perhaps by stray bullets, perhaps by a patrol. No one else dared to venture out.

The firing intensified toward evening. A sound like a heavy barrage came from the direction of the river and didn't stop until late at night. But it soon resumed and was eventually drowned out by the booming of cannon. People settled down in the basements. Some fell asleep as quickly as if they had been lying in their own beds. Others couldn't sleep, and still others were kept awake by their hunger. All the basements were overcrowded, because the poor, who had no basements, were, of course, taken in by the more prosperous Jews, who shared their food only with the children of the poor, because of the shortage. If the battle didn't end soon, everyone would starve to death.

I remember many episodes. Trivial and revealing details are inscribed so vividly in my memory that they have always been at my beck and call. Let me record a few of them here—although they are by no means intrinsic, not essential to explain how a very young person, a child like myself, is hurled out of his particular, individual life under the assault of events, so that the things he experiences during several hours or days are not *individualizing* for him. He experiences everything with the extreme intensity that seems to internalize every event. But he knows he is helplessly trapped in a life-threatening situation. Everything is extremely dangerous for him, but nothing threatens him alone; he could therefore be someone else or not exist at all.

The next morning, when my teacher left the basement to obtain food and medicine for a sick person in our midst, I followed him without my parents' noticing it. I had no trouble catching up with him, and together we walked through back streets, hugging the house walls so the soldiers wouldn't see us. There was a lull in the fighting now; the cannon were silent too. The teacher, who had been in the army and was also an intelligent man, always acting with due deliberation, decided to cut across the cemetery, partly because we could seek cover behind the gravestones. He was just explaining to me why Yiddish uses the Hebrew word *bes-oylem*, "house of the world" or "house of eternity," for the cemetery when the gunfire began again. It almost looked, the teacher said, as if the howitzers were being aimed at the Jewish graveyard. Which meant us, as we struggled through the deep snow. We ducked down behind headstones, to wait it out, concealing ourselves from the cannoniers across the river. But the shooting kept up, growing more and more violent. All at once, we heard a horse galloping behind us. We turned around: a small soldier, a Russian, came riding up, continuously lashing his huge mount with his whip. Suddenly, something happened, as horrible as only a nightmare can be: the horse's belly and the rider's torso were heaved up as if by an invisible force and ripped to shreds. Some of the pieces landed on the ground near us, staining the snow red. "Don't worry," my teacher whispered, "look the other way. Close your eyes and don't think, don't think about anything."

We heard wild shrieks rising from the river. They quickly came closer, then suddenly faded. But the booming of the cannon didn't stop, although there were fewer hits in the cemetery. My whole body quaked. We had to get up—nothing helped—and, seeking cover behind head-stones, we had to get out as fast as possible. We didn't walk—we ran, we leaped from grave to grave. We were near the small gate of the old wall when something exploded with a tremendous impact in front of us, among the fresh graves. I convulsively shut my eyes to avoid seeing the things that were hurled out of the ground. My terror paralyzed me, iron hoops squeezed my chest. "C'mon, c'mon! It's over!" I heard my teacher whisper. I wanted to say something, but only a pathetic whimper came out of my mouth. After a short while, we ran over toward the wall, tumbling into a crater that had probably been torn up by a grenade that night, for it was already covered by a thin layer of snow. There we remained, half-sitting, half-lying. My anguish gradually abated, and my legs stopped shaking. I had to pull my hands out of my coat pockets, slip off my gloves, and rub snow on my tear-stained face. It is written somewhere, said my teacher, that every living creature is afraid. The important thing, however, is to have the courage of your own fear, and to fear the murderer, not his shadow. Nor your own shadow. I nodded at everything, overly eager, though I wasn't sure whether I really under-stood. I just wanted him to keep talking, on and on. His words didn't ward off the cannon, but they shielded us against fear, that dreadful, paralyzing terror, whose recurrence I feared more at this point than the worst things that had ever happened to me.

Without discussing it, we began running again, leaping, although we were no longer protected by gravestones. We reached the wall and found the gate, which was ajar, not shut. We pushed it open and peered into the distance, toward the opposite river bank and the road, which led past the Christian houses to the railroad station. "This is the calm before the storm." That was how my teacher explained the deathly hush that had settled on everything. I couldn't remember when the shooting had stopped, I hadn't noticed. And I wanted to ask whether the calm before a storm meant anything special, and if so, what. But I was speechless, for I sensed the terror returning at that very instant—it would overpower me, and I would no longer be I. Trembling, I realized I still didn't have the courage of my fear.

"Don't look around, that's better, and start walking on your right foot!" my teacher ordered. So we were going to return empty-handed. Above us, to the right, lay the cemetery. I only gazed straight ahead or watched the river meadows to the left and the old houses lining them. Nothing stirred, but you could see spots in the snow; they might be shot-up wagons, dead soldiers or horses. I just wanted to be careful, remain on the barely visible path, behind my teacher, who had a hard time advancing. But I couldn't help looking again and again toward the meadows. Suddenly, we heard noises, shouts, the whinnying of horses. The din came from the marketplace, right behind the bridge. We threw ourselves into the snow. Soon, the horsemen appeared—Austrian lancers, with infantrymen dashing behind them. They held their rifles with bayonets in firing position. No sooner had they passed the final house than they encountered cross fire. It came from the Russians, who had concealed themselves in the trenches on either side of the station promenade.

Again my teacher told me to shut my eyes and not be afraid, for we weren't in the firing line and the whole thing could last only a couple of minutes. But I was unable to shut my eyes, so I looked away. Yet, virtually against my will, I kept staring over and over at the commotion. Finally, my teacher said, "We mustn't lose another moment!" We leaped up and didn't stop running until we were home.

The teacher was greeted joyfully by everyone; they had feared for his life. No one knew that I had gone with him. They had noticed my absence, but assumed I was in the basement next door. The teacher glanced at me, and I realized I shouldn't rock the boat. I couldn't eat that evening—I was afraid I'd vomit everything. Late that night, I woke up crying. My parents and the teacher stood around my bed. My father couldn't understand what had so completely unnerved a big, brave boy like me. Everyone else was enduring these difficult hours so well, whether in the basement or at home, except for me—me of all people! My father was completely perplexed. While they were trying to calm me down, the cannon started again. They had been right. The battle for the bridgehead and the shtetl was still raging. We descended into the basement again, probably for the last time, since the Austro-Hungarian army was advancing victoriously. Only a few hours more—and we'd be rid of the Russians and probably soon have peace again. Amen! everyone said.

Early the next day, a new violent barrage was launched. It seemed to go on forever, but it was all over by late morning. The Russians had been driven away—for good, people thought.

Everyone poured into the streets. They went to the river; fallen soldiers were still lying there, each one where a deadly bullet had struck him down. A young soldier lay near the blown-up bridge. He looked as if he were asleep and had wept in his sleep. No wound was visible on him, no blood. People stood around him, and an old peasant woman wept. A few minutes later, when Doino approached the corpse again, he noticed that the dead man's shoes were gone as was the wretched portfolio that had been in his top outside pocket. And it was only now that Doino wept too—not from grief for the young soldier, but from rage at the living, from deep shame.

Measured by the overall events of the war, the skirmishes I have just mentioned were so insignificant that they probably wouldn't be worth mentioning except in a battalion chronicle. Indeed, during the next eighteen months, I was to witness far more important events. Yet for a long time now, there has been no question for me that in those early months of the year 1915, when our shtetl was ravaged by epidemics and warfare, my childhood found its abrupt end and my life took a turn that would subsequently regulate and sometimes even dictate all aspects of my development. During those days and nights, especially during the few hours in the cemetery and then during the charge, I went through a break, and its effect was permanent. After those experiences, I never again saw the world in the same way: as a totality whose shining image was endlessly reflected in two facing mirrors. Now the mirrors had splintered and partly dimmed—they showed nothing whole anymore, only fragments.

What could I grasp back then of everything that had happened to us, to me? Not very much, of course. But a lot more than one would normally expect of an intelligent ten-year-old boy. Profoundly shaken, I realized that there was no protective heaven over human beings, all they have, all we have is the earth, the boundlessly indifferent, oblivious world. The most profound effect came when I began to think *we* instead of *I*. We, that is, not just my family, not just our nation, but we human beings in the face of something that, both murderous and indifferent at once, determined our lives—that is our deaths. And this something was not God. Had the messenger ridden by one second earlier, the howitzer would still have exploded, but everything would have been different. Thus, destiny was blind, so you had to be against destiny and do everything you could to make us ourselves our own destiny. Clay in the potter's hand, that was what was written. What, were we supposed to be clay in the hand of a *blind* potter? I now thought *we,* as I have said, not *I,* because I had been forced to watch human beings sweep up like a storm from afar, charge one another, kill and die. And none of them had done it as an *I*—that was the most improbable aspect, and yet it was true. Not one had died his own death, as the I that he was.

Back then, I would never have formulated these things in this way, of course. But that's beside the point. Henceforth, I knew that the world looked as it was reflected by the half-faded, splintered mirror, and I knew it had to be changed; and that only a we, not an I, could change it.

The end of a childhood spells a deep, far-reaching change. But this did not mean that I lost my interest in myself or that I discarded my intricate egotism. And for many years, I was still able, if more and more seldom, to enjoy myself like a boy and give in to illusions, foolishly exaggerating expectations and anxieties. In this way and in so many others, I was still my old self and like other boys my age; yet I clearly understood that I had fallen out of the nest. During the minutes in which the slaughter had taken place, and then the next day, when I saw the plundered corpse again, I was overwhelmed by a strange desire: In that din and in my unspeakable fear, I had felt as if I heard myself narrating the events to someone—as the memory of a much earlier experience. I was virtually *making the present recede* by projecting myself into a remote future time when I would describe something as past that was actually an inundating, overpowering present.

This strange future projection has never left me. I did not try to find an explanation for it until much later; no explanation was fully satisfying. The danger and horror of the adult world had rushed into my life with an inescapable force. Although it happened to me for the first time, the evil was by no means unfamiliar to me; I had heard or read about it all—for instance, in the Bible. There, it had affected me, but not endangered me; I hadn't been terrified that the earth below me might plunge into nothingness or rise into nothingness—simply because it was only an account, a story. But now, after those events, I did the opposite: I transformed what I was experiencing into a later account. In this way, I obtained the subjective assurance that I would survive: "And I alone escaped to report this to you, Job."

This explanation is not wrong, but inadequate, because it leaves out certain things that are probably important. For example, the terror I have just described, caused by violence, destroyed the image I had gradually developed—partly under my father's influence—of myself and my fearlessness. During those events, I lost faith in my steadfastness and became distrustful of my own self. The following night, when I tried to comfort myself after my crying jag, I told myself there could be no steadfastness against the immensity of the violence, especially in the cannon fire, for it would not help much. But it was not until decades later that I was able to examine the relationship between violence, terror, anxiety, and fear, between courage, discouragement, and lack of courage. Now I am resigned to the insight that all psychological explanations and interpretations are fragmentary in regard to the essence. I will therefore let the matter rest for now with the assumption that the threatened body can seek refuge in a distant space and the terrified mind in a coming time— thanks to that strange withdrawal from the present.

The shtetl still wasn't liberated even after those skirmishes, for a few days later, a Russian counterattack succeeded. At the last moment my family fled to Kolomea, the nearby capital of our province. The situation was unstable for several weeks. Finally, the Russians withdrew far enough along our sector, so that we returned home. At last, spring came, and the epidemics vanished, although more slowly than people had hoped. It was not easy recognizing the girls and young women who showed up with almost bald heads in the streets. We got used to the pocked faces of the people who had survived smallpox. No one suffered from the cold anymore, the shtetl had somewhat better supplies. The Viennese newspapers came again, and so did letters from America, albeit seldom, with dollars and sepia-colored photos. People repaired their wooden houses, which had been partly destroyed. Headstones were placed where they belonged. The fresh graves of those who had succumbed to the epidemic were marked by small boards. That would have to suffice for the moment, people said, everything would be done properly in peacetime.

Units withdrawing from the front kept stationing themselves in our shtetl or in the surrounding villages—for several days or weeks. The babel of tongues in the Austro-Hungarian army made communicating with the soldiers difficult, sometimes dangerous. The biggest problem was with the Hungarians, whose language none of us understood. The soldiers quickly lost patience, but eventually we communicated in that peculiar military German of which nearly every soldier knew a few snatches. A miserable barter flourished: the soldiers had no money, so they paid with their food rations, pieces of their uniforms, shoes, tobacco, and the like. In dark back streets, they met Jewish and Christian girls, as well as young war widows, buying their favors with food or a few crowns. Everything was done standing. I must have walked past the couples now and again. Those things may have struck me, but not shaken or especially moved me. That's part of the war too, people said in the shtetl. And we knew from the Bible that prostitutes had always existed. The women consorting with the foreign men, who had been separated from their wives for such a long time, were nearly always the poorest of the poor— constantly seeking food for their children, themselves, and their orphaned brothers and sisters. The shtetl, usually so terribly strict, refused to condemn them; people looked the other way.

And then, toward summer, we heard that the Russians had unexpectedly broken through somewhere along the Dniester. Early in the morning, the large marketplace was crowded with soldiers, most of them lightly wounded; the seriously wounded were in farm wagons in the square, in all streets, and on the periphery of the shtetl. Then came officers in automobiles, and military police units. A major ordered the mayor to evacuate the shtetl completely by 5 P.M. As usual, we were among the last to flee. When we were on the other side of the river, we heard the explosions that wiped out entire streets. It turned out later that this systematic demolition was utterly useless.

The next night, as I have already described, I thought I kept seeing wooden stairs in front of a white house. This seductive, confusing, ultimately depressing illusion disappeared when morning came. We had left the forest; the stone road led past a large, flat area. And there we all saw it—this time it was no optical illusion: a shiny silver airplane, the first we had ever seen up close, on the ground. The pilot stood next to it, dressed in light-brown leather from head to foot: a very tall young man, smoking cigarettes with long, gold tips. He would take only a few puffs, then throw the cigarette at the feet of the onlookers, draw a gold cigarette case from his breast pocket, and remove another cigarette, which he lit with an automatic lighter.

A few minutes later, it was time: he boarded the plane. While he pulled his leather helmet over his head, a soldier swung the propellor. We all stepped back. I sat down in the grass, not the least bit tired or sleepy, but strangely awake. We saw the plane taxi across the field and finally lift up shakily. It circled twice over our heads in a ribbon of sunbeams. Then the gilded craft soared off in the direction of the booming cannon. Had I already known the Nietzschean word *superman*, I would have used it for that aviator. I would have liked to stay until his return to watch him land, but also to see whether such a man moved on the ground just like anyone else.

We traveled on, reaching Kuty, a small town, for which, incidentally, our province, the poorest and most backward in Galicia, was named: Prokucie. It was Friday, and we wanted to remain here to celebrate the Sabbath. But our hosts were preparing to flee across the nearby border into Bukovina, for it looked as if the Russians, who were cornered on the main front in Galicia, would be attacking all the more vigorously in this secondary theater of war in order to make a breach in the Austrian positions. So we continued our flight, again among the stragglers. The mountain roads were quite narrow, but not too steep, and they were sound and dry. Evening set in. The women remained in the wagons drawn by one or two horses; thus, for the first time in their lives, they broke the prohibition against riding on the Sabbath. But they too got out when, after a bend in the road, we saw something that left us all dumbstruck. Before us, the road ascended in several loops, and we could make out the edges because they were illuminated by tiny flames flickering back and forth in the faint breeze. We all understood that these were Sabbath candles, which Jewish women since time immemorial have been lighting every Friday, just before evening, while speaking a blessing. We moved on, past these candles, as if they were the trophies of a victory—a victory not just over the enemies on earth, but also over God, who had once again been prevented from turning his face away from his people, from these lost, aimlessly fleeing, completely defenseless inhabitants of a Hasidic shtetl.

Toward midnight we reached the place that was the terminal station of a mountain railroad line. Although his home was crowded with refugees, our host took us in as if he had been looking forward to our visit all his life. Yet it was obvious that we would have to move on the very next morning, since the front was approaching inexorably. There were railroad cars at the station. If a locomotive came, we could flee to southern Bukovina and find a safe haven at last.

We boarded the cars in the first rays of dawn; the locomotive was not long in coming. Riding a train meant once again breaking a strict Sabbath law. We were sad, indeed horrified; but an exception could be made since we were doing it to save human lives. No sooner had the train lumbered off than all the men gathered in one car for worship. They prayed so fervently that while they didn't forget the mortal danger threatening them and their families, they nevertheless drew hope that the Almighty would not refuse to save them.

We spent almost two months in the beautiful sprawling village with clean white houses, where my father's only brother lived with his wife. For us children, it was like a wonderful vacation. We climbed around in the mountains; we fished in the mountain brook, catching as much as we needed.

In the autumn, we returned home. The enemy had left our shtetl several weeks earlier—he would never come again, everyone kept repeating confidently. The front of our house had been pitted by countless shots, but we could settle in comfortably. Fall had come early; it was cold, but less rainy than usual. The children were *learning* again, for the teachers and parents said we had so much catching-up to do. Every week brought a new peace rumor; people were fooled because they needed hope like a piece of bread. Life was terribly hard, much harder than anyone would have thought possible. Large portions of the country were still occupied; the coal mines and oil wells and the provinces that were rich in grain were inaccessible to us.

People were slow to forget the victims of the epidemics, but they did forget them, for now we gradually learned the names of the fallen soldiers, whom the shtetl had to mourn, and the names of the critically wounded, who lay in hospitals somewhere and might never come back. What would the widows and orphans live on? What would become of the brides whose fiancés were dead or—perhaps even worse—crippled?

The Hasidim who had traveled to their rabbi during the autumn holy days hinted mysteriously that we could be as good as certain that the Messiah was on the way. Redemption was approaching with giant steps; the era of the Messiah had already begun—for otherwise it would make no sense that this war kept spreading further and further every day, so that ultimately all the nations on earth would be driven together to the slaughtering block. It was incomprehensible that people had to starve, even in autumn, when the harvest is in the barns, that people had to freeze, even though there were more trees than ever, because the wood-cutters had been turned into uniformed killers. It was incomprehensible that sons were bleeding to death and not mourned by their parents, not carried to their graves by their families, because everything was happening in the darkness of minds and nocturnal ignorance, which spreads everywhere before the great, the everlasting light shines upon the world and all its abysses.

The irony remained as inevitable and obtrusive as ever, but it was more saddening than cheering: "You laugh—woe unto you and your laughter!" Someone might mumble that to himself after coming out with a *git-vertl*, a quip, and laughing at it. Still, it was taken for granted that the catastrophe was merely a transition. During that harsh winter, I often heard people repeating, "If the Messiah doesn't come now, when should he come?" But I was already ten years old; my apprenticeship with sly little Berele and his headstands lay way, way back. I was still religious, of course, but in a different way. Everything had a purpose and meaning, a manifest one and a secret one. Yes, everything. But not war, not this nonstop murdering, not this misery. I did not know the word *absurd,* but it alone expresses what I thought back then about the permanent catastrophe in which everything was caught. I sometimes lulled myself to sleep, repeating over and over again, almost inaudibly, as if it were a lullaby: It makes no sense, it makes no sense.

I probably could have mustered the courage to ask my great-grandfather what sense this senselessness made. Perhaps I could have asked him to justify what was happening. But he had died one year before the war. My great-grandmother had found him at his desk one morning, his head on his books, the large, red handkerchief in his cramped hand. . . . Strange that I didn't ask my father this question. I was on my own. People viewed me as a very sad child, who always looked for solitude, with or without a book in his hand. But I wasn't really sad, merely pensive in a particular way. I understood that I didn't understand very much, and I knew that I knew far too little. I had thought about such things earlier, and I had eagerly looked forward to everything I still had to learn. But now I felt I could no longer believe in the usefulness of knowledge. My eagerness was gone—forever, I feared.

In those days, I rebelled for the first time against one kind of knowledge: the study of the Talmudic tractate *Gitin,* from which I was supposed to acquire everything worth knowing about divorce. The explanations, which were supposed to make me see the light, struck me as weak, even ridiculous; and besides, I sensed that my father and my teacher, who wanted to persuade me, were not unshakably convinced themselves. I would probably have found any other tractate uninteresting; so it wasn't that the divorce laws of ancient Israel didn't interest me. Many years later, I would read several volumes of the Talmud in a German translation and, much later, take part in the fight against the enemies of the Talmud, which is certainly one of the most slandered works in history.

Between our homecoming in fall 1915 and our fourth and last flight in early summer 1916, many things happened, with drastic effects on our daily lives. But I no longer experienced them as a child. They were no longer *fleeting eternities*; they were events which were not interrupted even when they stopped. I realized we were in the middle of a river that flowed through many countries, making you think it had completely changed its direction over and over again. Sometimes it flowed along peacefully, but suddenly it plunged down foaming waterfalls; yet it was the same river, and there was no stopping. Man comes from dust and goes back to dust, our prayers said, and his return to dust begins in the moment of his birth.

Eventually, I rediscovered some of the things that happened back then, and I will talk about a few of them later on. For many years I was to live in deep intimacy with death. I feared death then a lot more than, say, now, when my old age brings me closer to it every day. But at the same time, I thought that we were forced to gamble with death, play a game that death would ultimately never lose. Always, and in everything, I was certain of the help I would get from my family and, in an emergency, even from strangers. It was only in regard to death that I felt alone, all alone, ever since that incident in the cemetery. And where was God? And what good was his omnipotence for him, for us?

In our final flight, we at last reached the Hungarian-Galician border in the Carpathians after numerous detours. Here we had an accident that could have been fatal. One of the horses suddenly got skittish and pulled the wagon to the right. The wagon, too wide for the narrow path, now tottered on the edge of the abyss. The horse slipped, lost its hold, and yanked the other horse along. The second horse reared up in terror, got tangled in the reins, and dangled over the brink. A tiny sapling blocked the left wheel of the wagon, so we could all jump out. Woodcutters had noticed the accident and dashed over to help us. Still, it took hours before we could get underway again. Late that night, we reached the shtetl where an uncle of my father had taken over the rabbinate that my great-grandfather Borekh had given up long ago in his deep resentment. We remained here for only a few days, even though this area seemed to be protected against the Russian invasion (and it was in fact spared). My memory of my great-uncle's house is still vivid for a special reason— indeed, it has always stayed with me, as a meaningful warning and also as shame at an unforgivable, senseless self-denial.

It may have happened the very night of our arrival: the rabbi began to converse with me and my fourteen-year-old brother as soon as we were alone with him. Instead of expressing his sympathy, he used my father's absence to rebuke us, but the reproaches were actually aimed at my father. He explained our situation, the loss of our home, the long, difficult flight, and even the accident, from which we still hadn't recovered—all these things, the rabbi declared, were God's just punishment for our sins. He alluded especially to the fact that my brother, who had been attending the Polish high school, desecrated the Sabbath every time he wrote there on that day, thereby betraying all Judaism. Our sufferings were also caused by the fact that our father and his children did not wear sidelocks and probably neglected to pray very often. Everything was connected, said our great-uncle, the angry rabbi, who, incidentally, became chief rabbi in Rumania just a few years later. My brother Hesio, who was usually not argumentative, but friendly and accommodating, spoke back, at first hesitantly, but then more and more firmly. We were both exhausted, but the insult drove away his fatigue; he stood his ground forcefully, losing any fear of the strict man.

"But you, you know I'm right!" our host suddenly addressed me, after previously ignoring my presence. I kept silent because I didn't believe this at all. But he kept driving away at me. I had to answer. We were in his home, we had eaten at his table, and we were supposed to spend the night here. It was hard for me to disagree with him as my brother had done; I was afraid of acting ungrateful and unseemly, since he was an important person commanding respect. My brother too now looked at me expectantly, certain that I shared his opinion. I finally opened my mouth, confessing our sinfulness, stuttering that it had caused all our misery, just as the rabbi claimed. Our great-uncle had probably taken over our great-grandfather's severity and probably a great deal of knowledge, but not his wisdom and not his austere kindness. I lowered my eyes to avoid my brother's look, for I was ashamed of my answer, of my toadyism and cowardice.

Throughout my life, I have been faced with many similar ordeals since that one, and I don't think I have ever expressed any false opinions from intimidation or some personal expediency. Whenever I felt like giving in and, for whatever reason, admitting as a truth something I did not regard as such, I immediately recalled that scene, which I felt ashamed about for many long years. As I grew older, I sometimes felt entitled to remain silent if my contradiction was bound to be useless. But I have never held my tongue for the sake of mental comfort or opportunism. Thus I, a nonbeliever, have remained true to my great-grandfather, more true, possibly, than all the rabbis who have descended from him.

But now it is really time to say farewell to the shtetl, as I have announced several times. On that July 27, 1916, when we got off the train at Franz-Joseph Terminal in Vienna, I was exactly ten years and seven months old. I did not think, I had no inkling, that there would be no return for me. Nor did I even ask about it, for I was absolutely certain that we had now finally reached the place with the gigantic gateway through which I would step into a wide world dedicated to the future. Everything lay before us.

No, I did not forget the shtetl in the following years and decades, which took me so far away from it that I felt as if it were on a different planet.

Perhaps my sense of being uprooted would never have developed if Hitler's victories had not led to that series of catastrophes which now seem as immediate as if twenty-seven years had not passed since his death. If the Jewish shtetls still existed today, they would belong, for me, only to a remote past. But since they were destroyed, so thoroughly wiped out that nothing of what they were or could have become can reach into the future, Zablotow now belongs to my present. It is at home in my memory.

But before I had even learned that Zablotow and the other shtetls no longer existed, I experienced a profound, an overwhelming loss that I could not define initially. I was living in Paris; it was a Friday evening in March 1938. I had switched on the radio, hoping to learn something about the front lines of the Spanish Civil War. Quite unexpectedly, I heard the announcer of Radio Cité say that Austria's fate was sealed— German troops were expected to march into Vienna during the next few hours. I found the Viennese station and listened for many hours, until late at night. I thus heard first-hand the demonstration of the masses that spilled over to the Ballhaus from all sides, mobbing the entire Heldenplatz. *"Sieg heil! Heil Hitler! Sieg heil!"* These shouts relentlessly permeated the shabby room of my miserable *hôtel garni*. That night, for the first time, I was overpowered by the peculiar sense of forlornness that accompanies an uprooted life. Naturally, I was afraid for my entire family and for so many friends who should have left Austria long ago but hadn't, because they couldn't tear themselves away from Vienna. I discovered to my amazement that I no longer perceived Vienna as the city that had become inaccessible to me (who could say for how long), like Berlin since 1933. No, I felt that Vienna would now have to vanish from the scene. That night I was orphaned; I lost my roots. I ordered myself not to feel homesick for the city that I had so boundlessly admired while I had still been in the shtetl, and that I had begun to love truly passionately, after it had disillusioned me as if by an evil spell—when Vienna's decline during the final years of World War I had warped it so deeply that it barely resembled its former self. Just what can this be: a boy's passionate love for a city whose grandeur and glory he had infinitely admired from afar and whose wretched decline he had to experience and to endure for countless days and nights?

"He knew this city too well, the way one knows a woman whom one no longer loves," I mentally wrote to Vienna—twenty-five years after that July 27, 1916, when I first set foot on Viennese soil. At that time, fall 1941, I was living near Nice. When I peered through the small window, I saw a tiny bay and, farther out, the smooth surface of the ocean glowing in the sun, and an olive grove, to the left, on an outjutting hill. What a marvelous area! I admired it in every season, but I was certain I would never be as homesick for it as I was for Vienna, no matter where I happened to be, for many long years. Vienna, not Zablotow, which I had never loved, although that was where I had first experienced what it means to be at home somewhere.

PART THREE

End and Beginning

Those first few months in Vienna come back in a series of parallel memories, as if all my experiences had each been sharply distinct from the very start. There was the experience of "the red shoes," which force the person wearing them to dance without stopping. For many weeks, until late autumn, I was incapable of resisting the lure of the streets. I wandered restlessly through the city, especially the first, second, third, ninth, and twentieth districts.* At first, I was looking for something: imperial splendor, the beauty of daydreams, perfection.

The war had been going on for two years. In the morning, the summer sun bathed everything in golden light, leaving cracks and breaks in the shadow. Yet I wasn't quite sure what I really wanted to find, and I still don't know today. Often when embracing a woman, one is also seeking refuge from oppressive, torturous disappointment found with the very woman being held in one's arms. Similarly, almost every day brought new disappointments with Vienna: Nevertheless, I did not stop looking, with my eyes wide open to the bridges, the streets, and the most out-of-the-way nooks, as well as the people: their faces, gestures, clothes; finally the palaces, the patrician mansions, the monuments. I was always attentive to the street noises, the songs, the music of the hurdy-gurdies, which

*[Trans. note: the first district was the center of Vienna, adjacent to the third district, which contained the Stadtpark; the second district was heavily Jewish; the ninth district was the university area; and the twentieth, adjacent to the second district, was inhabited by poor people, both Christian and Jewish.]

one often heard in the poorer areas. I wandered because I was searching, but probably also because I wanted to get away.

My second series of experiences during those months began the day we finally reached Vienna, with our plunge into poverty. We were soon to discover how deeply one can plunge. You believe you've hit bottom, but after a brief pause you fall even deeper. *Deeper than the Abyss.* That was the title of one of my novels. A critic protested, "There's no such thing. The abyss itself is the deepest depth." But between 1916 and 1918, sinking from level to level, I was to find out in endless detail, that every fall can trigger a further, deeper fall, and that the abyss has no bottom.

In the middle of the first night (we had been lodged in a miserable rooming house), we were awakened by my mother. In the dim light of a tiny electric bulb, she stood by our beds, horror and despair on her face. She pointed at the nearby wall and the ceiling and repeated: "Bedbugs, for God's sake, there are bedbugs here!" Her bewilderment made me feel that bedbugs (I knew they were insects but I had never seen any) were something very dangerous. My mother was a very intelligent woman, and courageous in perilous situations. Naturally, she was not unfamiliar with vermin; the poor people in the shtetl and in the surrounding countryside had been afflicted with fleas and lice and with cockroaches in their kitchens. Perhaps my mother panicked because this was the first time she had ever been awakened by bedbugs. But at that same moment, she must have realized that now, like the poor, we were defenseless—vulnerable to any kind of degradation caused by external circumstances. For her, this minor experience was the first sign of humiliation. And she wasn't wrong. The very next day, in a neighboring street, we rented two rooms from a married couple with many children. They were completely uneducated people; they fought with one another day in day out; their language was a mixture of curses, obscenities, and maledictions; their apartment was incredibly neglected and crawling with bedbugs. We didn't get our own apartment until autumn. We found this place in an indescribable condition. But we lacked the wherewithal to turn it into a home; this came only gradually. My parents left this apartment twenty-three years later, the day after the outbreak of World War II.

Our situation could have improved tremendously if my father had accepted a position in one of the major banks, consistent with his professional knowledge. But he refused, because he would not violate the Sabbath (in those days, Saturday was a normal workday).

My parents managed emotionally to endure their material decline, which was triggered by the war and accelerated by the food rationing and the profiteering. In our immediate vicinity there were thousands of refugees in a similar situation. It was too wretched to endure, which was why people once again drew that half-ironic, yet effective comfort from the certainty that the deepest fall could not be anything but the preliminary stage of the new ascent, and that the worst meant the virtually dialectical beginning, so to speak, of the improvement.

As in the shtetl, our door was always open, visitors popped in and out at all times, we seldom went to bed before midnight. The coal sufficed for heating just one single room, the smallest. The overcrowding in this tiny space did not interfere with the socializing. The tea, which kept growing weaker, was sweetened with saccharin, and glass after glass was drunk. The discussions were usually vehement, but people seldom fought because a quip was always interjected, in time to relieve the tension. My parents and their visitors could easily imagine that, on the one hand, nothing had changed for them and that, on the other hand, this situation could not last.

For me, this experience of total impoverishment, utterly blameless misery, was uniquely important. Today, as I recall that plunge and the inevitable, immediate consequences of that thoroughly degrading misery, I wonder how I realized that someday this misfortune would look like a special favor.

Berele and others like him, the overwhelming majority of the shtetl children whom I had seen at school, in synagogue, and on the street, had lived in a constant state of want. Their most urgent needs were met, but they almost never had enough, qualitatively or quantitatively. They and their families were subject to the cruel *domination of lack*. If Berele finally did receive a pair of shoes, they weren't new; they had been worn out by his older brother, and they were crooked and too large. There was a nasty proverb: "By the time the poor are allowed to dance, the musicians have to take a piss." And people quoted the ironic lament of the unlucky man: "If I sold candles, the sun wouldn't set anymore, and if I sold winding-sheets, people would stop dying."

I had always thought I knew everything about the poor, and now, at the age of eleven, my everyday life continually taught me what poverty is—really is, not just what it looks like to others. I had to take the trolley to carry an important message to someone who lived far away. When I started back, I realized I had lost one heller, which meant I couldn't pay my fare. I had to get out and walk all the way home through the suburbs.

I felt as if the conductor and a few of the passengers gazed at me with mocking satisfaction. I was offended, if only for an instant. But I realized that because a poor man has at best the barest necessity, the tiniest loss— a heller, for example—is a punishment. Granted, this was no new or deep insight; but I acquired it at the highest cost, by experiencing it personally.

About a year later, I received a pair of new shoes for the high holidays. The next day, during the tumult of a soccer game, I lost a heel without noticing it immediately, and then I couldn't find it. I was devastated, for I knew what a hard time my parents had buying clothes for us children. I came home very late; walking without one heel was difficult, and besides, I had timidly put off the moment when I had to confess to them that my exuberance had provoked this mishap. They should have reproached me bitterly; I thoroughly deserved it. But they didn't scold me, they even comforted me, for they noticed how dejected I felt. They realized that the poor always buy far worse and more expensive goods than anyone else, not only in wartime, but also in peacetime, when there are no shortages. That was a lesson I shouldn't forget, they said, even when conditions were back to normal and our circumstances were good again.

Our radical impoverishment (and not only that) made me begin to see everything around me, especially the people in the street, differently from before: I saw each person in his special manner: the way he walked, the look on his face, the clothes he was wearing. And this did not change, for I am still as attentive as ever to all people who cross my path. Aside from my need to see—almost a physical need, a sort of visual hunger—that situation in Vienna is still exerting its influence. It fostered my feeling of what might be called "naked humanity," which is neither humanitarianism nor its opposite, but an incapacity to remain indifferent to anything concerning human beings—primarily their existence. In the shtetl, in any small village, no one you run into is really a stranger, aside from visitors. In a big city, the reverse is true: people who are not strangers are the exception. I walked through the streets of the metropolis, unable and unwilling to resign myself to this strangeness. Even when I accepted the fact that other people weren't interested in me, weren't concerned about me, I nevertheless felt that they all concerned me.

This is not as odd as it may sound. What I have hinted at rather than described are motives that impelled not only me to become a Socialist. Why? Because I viewed people and their lives, their poverty and careworn existences as concerning me personally. The distinctions in class and social level cried for attention, becoming more and more blatant and outrageous every day the war went on. As a restless but not tireless wanderer, I often had to relax on benches or stairs, especially by the bridges, on the steps leading down to the banks of the Danube Canal. I was seldom alone; some elderly gentleman or a woman would always join me. Like me, they only wanted to rest briefly and then continue on their way because someone was waiting for them. And sometimes they wanted to leave precisely because no one in the whole world was waiting for them, no one needed them. Often enough, after standing up, such a woman would sink back on the bench and start a conversation with me because I was her only neighbor. They expected a boy to make at best terse replies and be all the more attentive to a monologue. My bench neighbor usually began by mentioning her increasing difficulties in breathing when she walked, the uncertainties of the weather, the insolent profiteering of the endless number of middlemen, who were growing rich at the expense of the poor, the shortage of goods, which only the rich people, the black marketeers, could afford. Then she would tell me about her family, about sons who had marched off, been wounded, were missing, or were furloughed, about daughters who had to work like men, for instance as streetcar conductors, or daughters-in-law who were carrying on shamefully as if they were already war widows.

Chance had brought these people close to me for a few minutes, and I listened to them, genuinely attentive, but seldom curious. I was already familiar with the things they told me, or else the details were trivialities that kept recurring. On the other hand, I was always impressed by their tone of voice, which revealed either resigned patience or angry impatience, the expectation or fear of imminent changes. The tone might suddenly shift right in the middle of an overly detailed, banal account of an everyday event. The voice might evince a bitterness that made a deeper impact on me than a shriek of despair, but the words to express them never came out. The narrator would go mute for an instant, then quickly stand up and leave, or else wipe everything away with a gesture, adding a few banal sentences.

Those were my first contacts with lower-class people. It was from them that I most frequently heard words and idioms of the Viennese dialect. Sometimes my bench neighbors would mix anti-Semitic comments into their reflections, expressing derision, hatred, and occasionally envy. During the first few weeks, I reacted to such comments as if they were personal insults and, my face grim, I would leave the enemy, not without proudly identifying myself as a Jew. Eventually, while I did not become more tolerant of these intolerant people, I tried to discuss the matter with them. To my surprise, I discovered that they didn't know any Jews personally; their hatred was constant, but quite superficial, and, strange as it may sound, it was a *frivolous* hatred.

Neither the Ruthenians in our area nor the Jews in our shtetl were frivolous. Thus in Vienna at the start of the third year of the war, I met frivolous people for the first time. They obviously waxed most eloquent when they spoke about any kind of pleasure. They tended to refer to any people who didn't belong with them as "out-of-towners," putting them down and waving them off disparagingly if not scornfully. The Viennese word *teppert*, stupid, was the one most frequently used in these conversations.

But what gave me the most to think about was the way they talked about the war. While they grieved for their relatives who had died in action, and while they felt sorry for the young invalids one encountered everywhere, it was painfully obvious that they knew nothing about the horrors of the war or—more accurately—preferred to know nothing.

The third set of experiences, which I mentioned earlier, was perplexing and extremely astonishing. It both stunned me and made me indignant, for reasons I could only gradually put into words. But this didn't occur until I was no longer alone. What happened was that I met a boy who had experienced the war directly, with a camouflaging, a sublime and uplifting mystification, which the entire city appeared to be practicing incessantly. The enthusiasm for the war, which was uninterruptedly blazoned forth, propagated, drummed in, drilled in by countless newspapers in the morning, afternoon, and evening, was, in my eyes, a gigantic, heinous *komedye*, with everyone joining in. The saddest sham ever to challenge your mind and your decency.

As eloquent as I may have been for my age, I did not have enough words at my command to express why and how excessively unbearable, inhuman, and inhumane I found this enthusiasm. It was the first time I was overwhelmed by a sense of suffocation along with disgust and outrage. Hardly a day went by without extra editions coming out and being hawked by countless vendors. They ran through the streets, yelling out the headlines almost nonstop; the glaring letters on the front pages announced victories—as well as the deaths of ten, twenty, fifty thousand soldiers, who "cover the battlefield as far as the eye can see."

You heard and read about the "golden hearts of the Viennese" everywhere. Hardly any of my garrulous bench neighbors failed to mention those hearts of gold—with that peculiar sigh of self-admiration—and yet it was the Viennese who pounced on the extra editions and their bloodthirsty articles. Their demand for foreign corpses was even greater than the mass-murder supply of the press with its lies and exaggerations. That was how I saw it, for I still hadn't discovered certain highly important things—not only because I was very young, but because I came from a highly spiritual milieu that was seldom influenced by urban civilization, and then only peripherally and belatedly. I didn't realize one could read triumphal reports on the deaths of thirty thousand innocent young men with joyful excitement because it was offered as a sensation and also because one could not, or did not have to, imagine anything concrete: not even the final useless cry for help uttered by a dying young soldier. I did not realize that news reports could arouse acute feelings of satisfaction or grief about events that they shouted out and simultaneously concealed behind an opaque veil.

It took me a long time to understand all this—this and so many other things; but it took me even longer to get rid of the severity with which I had been taught to criticize, to judge everything without exception in the name of Justice. A new apprenticeship began for everybody, yet hardly anyone could be more eager to learn than I was at that time and still am. On my deathbed—if I have a lucid moment—I will think with ironical self-pity that the most important phase of my schooling could now commence if only my allotted time were extended.

I have just reread the preceding section—the first pages of the final chapter of my childhood memories—and I am increasingly astounded that they barely depict the profound emotional upheavals that overwhelmed me almost constantly during those early months in Vienna. The intensity of impressions kept me in a constant state of alertness that knew no bounds. I was carried off by the present in such an intense way that there was only one time. I experienced it in a changing rhythm: it either dashed by swiftly or else oozed by so slowly that it appeared to stand still.

Perhaps a child's or an adolescent's enthusiasm is not forgotten, but perhaps the aged man who recollects it is unable to render it as he experienced it so long ago. Many things happened to me in Vienna back then, and my memory has retained countless details with verifiable accuracy. The topographic precision that still urges itself upon me now, when I walk through the streets of Vienna, confirms my assumption that the intensity of my experience must have been unusual. The cobblestones have become obtrusive marks, which, after more than half a century, guide the stroller back to his past—almost as if one could return, as if the river could flow upstream, as if what happened long ago could again become a first experience: "Even today I could indicate down to the very decimeter the exact place on *Praterstrasse*, right near the Carl-Theater, where I suddenly realized that I ran into the Prater every day because I hadn't yet learned how to live on the ruins of an illusion."

Was I so feverishly alert because for the time being, for several months, everything was new for me? New, but not as I had hoped it would be, therefore disappointing? Did I become the restless wanderer because I was seeking something that would finally make my earlier daydream come true? Yes, that's what it was, but there was so much else too. The events followed each other uninterruptedly, the people selling the extra editions yelled out the latest bulletins: their shouts would make the air vibrate, especially in the afternoon and in the cool evening hours—sometimes woeful shouts, as if announcing the end of the world, sometimes defiant ones, as if these were the booming threats of an irresistible force. The headlines were mostly about victories or successful counter-attacks, sometimes about scandals involving the food shortage, the profiteering, and the corrupting racketeers, occasionally also about "peace feelers," which were talked about in neutral countries. The more blood was shed, and the more the nations had to suffer, the more tremendous the lie became.

Like the adults, but possibly even more intensely than they, I looked forward to the news that would change everything and make the future we were yearning for seem almost present. But I lost this hope early enough. I therefore began to read the evening edition of the Social-Democratic *Arbeiter-Zeitung* [Worker's Newspaper], which was usually only one page long. It was very cheap—I think it cost only one heller—and I trusted it because it wrote against the war so often and because each issue had lots of blank spaces. This meant that the censorship office had forced the publisher to kill numerous articles and bulletins that didn't appeal to officials who wanted to make everything seem attractive. As a result, this newspaper often had only half a page to offer the reader. We were disappointed but happy, for this confirmed that we were on the side of truth.

There is a special reason why I remember so precisely that dismal, rainy afternoon when the newsboys yelled out the ear-splitting bulletin that Prime Minister Count Stürgkh had been shot to death by Dr. Friedrich Adler while having lunch in the Meissl & Schaden restaurant. I was standing right on the corner of Schmelzgasse and Taborstrasse, the longest street in the second *Bezirk* [district], where most of the poorer Jewish population lived. The barely intelligible shouts of the vendors made people stop, buy a paper, and read it immediately, causing a tie-up on the sidewalk. As I tried to decipher the account of the incident, I felt a painful burning on the back of my neck, to the left, above the bone. I touched the spot: someone had put out a cigarette butt there. When I turned around, I saw a tall man, who looked at me mockingly, then pushed his way through the crowd and vanished. I tried to follow him, but it was very difficult, and I soon lost sight of him. He had probably slipped into the Hospital of the Merciful Brother. My sharp pain persisted, but it was almost more unendurable to have been gratuitously humiliated by a stranger. I peered around. No one seemed to have noticed the incident. Why had the man done it? He could be fairly certain that the boy in this Jewish neighborhood was Jewish. This explanation was probably correct, I thought, but not fully adequate.

I waited in vain at the hospital entrance; the man was nowhere to be found. Then I crossed the street and walked slowly toward the Danube Canal, but kept looking around. Now that I had pulled myself together, I realized I could have done nothing against this enemy. Not a single one of the hurrying pedestrians would have helped me. The pain was no longer unbearable, and my self-pity comforted me a bit before yielding again to indignation and a sense of humiliation. I walked over to the center of Vienna and stopped in front of the newspaper building, where the extra editions were hung out together with the regular ones. I carefully read through the extra edition, then the morning edition, which devoted almost an entire page to the murder of a poor, old servant by a burglar. A bad photo showed a careworn, overworked woman. I waited for the evening edition, which was soon displayed. The front page offered photos of the assassin and his victim, the prime minister, who had dissolved parliament, stubbornly refusing to let it convene again. Count Stürgkh looked just as everyone pictured him: a dignitary, an elderly, rather introspective gentleman, who knows he is being photographed for a newspaper. Friedrich Adler, however, did not seem at all like someone who could kill or even physically attack another human being. He looked similarly introspective, scholarly, and no longer young, a middle-aged man. I am not certain whether my memory is deceiving me, but I think his hat tilted forward and perched at an angle. As I read the many statements ascribed to waiters and other witnesses of the assassination, my eyes kept wandering to the face of the man who, just a few hours earlier, had shot this elderly gentleman, the prime minister of imperial Austria, killing him in cold blood, most likely after mature deliberation. I was only a few hundred yards from our building (near the Marienbrücke). Once again I felt the pain in the back of my neck, but now it seemed stronger. I looked forward to active sympathy and comfort from my family and our visitors, who must have been more numerous than usual. From out on the landing, I could already hear the many voices, louder than ever. Neither my parents, nor my brothers, nor the guests paid any heed to my entrance or my no doubt exaggeratedly woeful face. My attempts to make them focus on my injured neck and the incident at the corner of Taborstrasse failed miserably. Soon I myself was involved in the debate, which, although triggered by the assassination, was thoroughly unpolitical. Even Count Stürgkh was mentioned only peripherally, not without regret that he hadn't died peacefully in his bed. The conversation, ending only toward midnight, centered mainly on the Adler family. There was old Dr. Victor Adler, Comrade Doctor (as he was called by the Socialist workers throughout the country), a great man. Even the Kaiser, it was said, always treated him with respect. Such a man had certainly done everything to provide the best upbringing for his son Friedrich, who was also a doctor, perhaps even a professor. And now suddenly, the almost inconceivable horror: he had learned from an extra edition that he, the venerable Dr. Victor Adler, was the father of a murderer. And everyone kept repeating the word *nebbikh*, Yiddish for *alas*, and "The Good Lord, the Almighty, should preserve us from such a calamity!" No one neglected to recall the kaiser from time to time, that poor suffering man: his wife had been assassinated, his son had died in the prime of life, his nephew, the pretender to the throne, had been gunned down in Sarajevo, and now he had to endure this misfortune with the count. The debaters didn't refuse to show him sympathy, but they were deeply moved only by Victor Adler's situation. What could, what would, what must this unhappy father do now? This question agitated them vehemently, as if each person had to make a fateful decision before dawn.

That night, I fell asleep very late. I was troubled by the incident, of which I was constantly reminded by my pain (which had meanwhile been soothed by a salve). At the same time, I felt compelled to view myself in the role of the assassin, test myself to see whether I could have acted as Friedrich Adler had. And as usual, "I filled in the gaps": There he was, in his room, gun in hand. Had he wanted to, he could have hidden it somewhere, forgotten it. But he loaded it with live bullets and thrust it into his coat pocket. He could have decided to stay home that day, put off his plan for twenty-four hours. He left the house and his family as if he were going to meet a friend. He could have gone to the library or his café, read newspapers, talk to associates. He headed toward the restaurant where Count Stürgkh could be found every day at the same time. Yes, Adler was still free not to commit the assassination even after sitting down at a table next to the count. But Friedrich Adler walked toward a man whom he had been observing for more than an hour, drew his revolver, squeezed the trigger, and killed his victim. To carry out his plan, he needed not only courage, not only daring, but the highest degree of self-control, for—as the photo showed—far from being a violent man, a killer, Friedrich Adler was extremely sensitive.

I thought about all these things that night; I most likely framed my thoughts in different words. It was the first time I ever felt so close to and so remote from a perfect stranger. It was the first time I felt an almost unbearable anxiety that inspired an idea that was both temptation and hesitation—even repugnance. I saw myself in Friedrich Adler's place, but unlike him, shrinking from the deed, panicking and fleeing.

It was wartime; thousands, tens of thousands of people were dying every day. I myself had been a horrified, trembling witness to such actions and sufferings. And now there was a single victim, an elderly man who shared responsibility for the war and for many other things. And there was an assassin, who had killed; but this by no means made him a murderer. He was a human being who wanted justice and peace for all human beings. That was the situation, and yet it was extremely confusing. What, justice kills? An individual can decide to condemn someone to death and kill the man himself?

I had no answer to the question. I didn't know why that stranger had attacked me from behind, and I didn't know whether to forgive my parents for showing absolutely no sympathy with their humiliated and injured son.

Early one morning, one month later to the very day, for the first time I heard my father sobbing. His tefillin were already wound around his arm, but he kept breaking off his prayer. The eighty-six-year-old emperor, Franz Joseph I, had died after a reign of sixty-eight years. When my father noticed that I wasn't particularly saddened by the news of his death, he repeated: "Austria has died with him. He was a good emperor for us. Now everything will be uncertain! It is a great misfortune for us Jews!" I was shaken by my father's tears. The event had affected me, but not deeply. The successor had already mounted to the throne, and I didn't see why the old kaiser's death would spell the end of Austria, of a world. Only later did I understand that his death really did signify an end; much later, I realized that my father's profound grief had not been unfounded.

Everyone said that the funeral would be one of a kind. As it happened, I was all alone, among strangers, when I watched the unusual, colorful spectacle: first on Biberstrasse, then on Domikanerbastei, two streets rising parallel from the Franz Joseph Quai. (Both streets would become significant for me in later years.)

Dignitaries of every kind had poured into Vienna from all parts of the dual monarchy. As they marched by in their traditional garb, I almost forgot that this was the funeral procession for the kaiser, whose death my father was mourning. What we, the rows of curious onlookers, saw was a walking masquerade, whose participants aroused universal admiration with the splendor of their garments and embellishments. They trudged solemnly, of course, to the rhythm of a funeral march, but after many hours wore on, the spectators became less curious because the endless variety of costumes eventually grew monotonous. The cries of admiration died out; people felt tired after standing so long; it wasn't exactly warm out. Some may have wondered whether these privileged individuals in their ancient and pretentious wardrobe were more intent on displaying their power than showing their grief for the emperor.

I wasn't free of this suspicion, but I remained stationary for many hours, expecting that something would have to come, would have to follow in the end, to give some meaning to this beautiful but meaningless spectacle. The hours passed; nothing came. But something like that still happens to me frequently. While reading a book or watching a play, I may feel like giving up, but I don't, because I expect something will suddenly come on page 136 or toward the end of Act II, to lend a surprising and profound meaning to what has already happened and make everything that is still to come extraordinarily interesting. Although my hope is usually frustrated, it is renewed on every occasion.

So I held out until the end of the parade, only changing over to the next parallel street. Ultimately it must have been not useless but informative, like most of the unselfish follies we commit in our youth. That day, I realized that the decorative emphasis on rank, the flaunting of a position one has struggled to attain, can inspire only irony. While my weary eyes apathetically followed the procession of Magyar noblemen from Slovakia, I proudly thought of my great-grandfather, who had remained without any sign of rank, but whose dignity had always commanded respect from everyone, including Ukrainians and strangers. He despised all pretense, all inauthenticity, and more than anything he hated the most dangerous illusion: the mixture of genuine and ungenuine. And now I had seen the splendor of centuries march by. Ultimately, I had grown bored and discovered that such glory was unimportant because it can have only pseudo-significance.

At my home that evening, people mournfully talked on and on about the old kaiser, but not about the funeral rites. They feared no evil from his successor. Nor did they expect much of him. There was probably no one from whom much could be expected. It was very late, they said, too late. No one asked, no one said what it was too late for. . . . The year 1916 was waning. It seemed to have been filled with countless experiences, but I expected even more of the new year.

Meanwhile, something had changed in our home. My mother had to have an operation. Her mother, who had found refuge in Bohemia with her daughter from a different marriage and the daughter's family, came to us for several weeks in order to run the household. Grandmother Feygy had been divorced several times. Her daughter by her second husband, my mother, had grown up with her father, who had remarried very soon and then had seven daughters by his second wife. Bobe Feygy was an extremely intelligent, helpful, and energetic woman with a good sense of humor. She made her decisions tyrannically, never thinking that she might change them under someone else's influence. She felt that no one else could know better what she wanted—and that was all she cared about. Doing the right thing was something she took for granted. In her youth, she had been an unusually attractive woman, but far too independent in her thoughts and actions.

I owe her many informative hours, which have never lost their effect on me. On the surface these were banalities. We had no maid, of course, but my grandmother couldn't bend over, and many chores were too difficult for her. My older brother Hesio was a young man, almost fifteen, and my younger brother Milo only five. Therefore she couldn't ask anything of anyone but me. I was, so to speak, exactly the right age for her purposes: almost eleven. Her way of getting me to do the most varied chores was—intentionally or not—a methodical parody of my father's over-expectant attitude. When I was supposed to wash the floors, which were damaged in many places and rotting in others, Bobe Feygy could speak earnest words to me with kind mockery in her young eyes, making it clear that I was unbelievably skillful at washing and wiping the floor, so that she wanted *me* to do this work. For my part, I always or nearly always did what she wanted me to do. This time, it was no longer my old game, for she was, of course, far superior to Berele and knew that I realized she was using a trick. Furthermore, she never concealed her irony, and I knew that she knew that I knew . . . and so on, ad infinitum. It was only when she was sure I was available that she followed her compliment and request with the promise of a reward: ten or fifty hellers—sometimes, seldom enough, a whole crown.

A few years later, when I read the first few lines of *The Eighteenth of Brumaire,* in which Marx speaks about the recurrence of special events, I told myself with adolescent pride: I know a thing or two about that. The ironic game of the only seemingly disguised deception with which my grandmother parodied the overly enticing trust that my father placed in me was no repetition in the form of a farce; it was both a revelation and a liberation. It also destroyed the pretentious assurance of the secret superiority that a person thinks he has achieved, acting as if he didn't know he was being fooled. While slowly moving forward on my knees, trying to dry the floor with the miserable, threadbare rag, I couldn't help thinking of Berele. And I had a suspicion that he too might have known that I knew, but that he had hidden it from me just as I had hidden it from him. Wiping the floor, I learned never again to underestimate people.

After my mother recovered, Bobe Feygy left us, returning to Kolomea shortly before the end of World War I. I never saw her again. In 1939, when the Nazis conquered this city, which had been annexed by the Soviet Union, they shot many of the Jewish inhabitants here and in the surrounding shtetls. All the rest were transported to death camps, where they died. Inadvertently, the murderers overlooked an old bed-ridden woman, who lived all alone. Her few remaining neighbors, Christians, knew she was there, but didn't want to risk their lives by bringing her food. She starved to death, very slowly, however long it took to die like that. The old woman was my grandmother Feygy.

At the end of the year 1916, I thought that a new life would begin for me. I have often pinned similar hopes on a new year. However, it is true that I have often looked back to the year 1917 with special—how shall I put it?—with grim, defiant gratitude. In the course of those twelve months, barely a day passed without bringing something new. It began with a paying job. At lunchtime and suppertime, I performed a responsible function in a Jewish relief kitchen where my father worked as bookkeeper and cashier: I distributed silverware to the guests in exchange for a deposit, usually an ID card. When the diner brought back the knife, fork, and spoon, I returned his deposit and rinsed the cutlery in a bucket of lukewarm water before handing them out again. The patrons were not only the poorest inhabitants in this part of the second Bezirk, but also war invalids and soldiers on furlough, who vanished again after a few days or weeks. Often, breaking the rule, I had to give someone the cutlery without a cash deposit or a document, for there were always people who had neither. Aside from soldiers on leave, the majority of diners were steady customers, most of whom liked chatting with me if the place wasn't too crowded and I had time to listen. Thus, I got to know their names, their situations, their sufferings, and their hopes.

My job at the relief kitchen brought me pocket money that enabled me to attend the cheaper afternoon showing at a movie house at least once a week. I got to see the program announcements twice daily because the theater was on the way to my school. This depressingly dismal place, unclean and airless, was named after the Austrian playwright Johann Nestroy, who has made so many generations of Austrians laugh. It was opposite the Carl-Theater, where this dramatist, who is still unknown outside his homeland, had once been the foremost author and actor for many long years.

A few years before the war, an itinerant "cinematographer" had screened a movie in Zablotow, and we had watched it, astonished, of course, and admiringly. But in the year 1917, at the Nestroy Kino, I discovered the might and magic of film; my experience was varied and complex. The most lasting impact was made on me by the newsreel, especially the front-line reports, which, although edited and controlled as propaganda, transformed shattering events into visions—like dreams that jolt you awake and leave you feeling virtually "dead." In the usually half-empty theater, its front rows—the cheapest seats—occupied by yowling children, I was shown that the acts of war I had witnessed in Zablotow and on the endless roads of our escape had been nothing but tiny episodes. The firing of cannon and howitzers, as I now realized, was like a war game compared with the artillery battles filmed by the newsreel reporters. It was all silent of course. Sometimes there was a piano player, but his whimsically assembled music usually accompanied only the features. The images of ear-splitting events would therefore have unrolled in a deathly hush, if the spectators, mostly twelve- to fifteen-year-olds, hadn't created an infernal uproar. Actively taking part in the spectacle, hollering things they thought were witty, they goaded the artillerists to load faster, to keep shooting uninterruptedly. At the sight of prisoners of war, the boys outdid one another inventing abusive names, which they yelled at the screen. And if close combat was shown, they shouted themselves hoarse, participating intensely in the violence—they wanted so badly to be avengers, saviors, heroes.

During the first few performances that I watched, my heart hammering, my body sometimes trembling with terror and indignation, those blood-thirsty screamers filled me with profound scorn, even hatred. I despised their stupidity; I loathed their inhumanity. But gradually, after just a few weeks, the whole scene looked quite different to me. I realized I had misunderstood them. Their actions, their hubbub were basically a game that they not only enjoyed but needed as a shield against the anxiety, the fear aroused in them by the confusing, utterly alien events on the screen. They were no more cruel than readers of the extra editions who delighted in the high numbers of allegedly killed enemies. The readers and these boys perceived the horrifying reality only as the reflection of a reflection. They constantly mistook the shadow for the body casting it; their literal imaginations were inadequate for picturing what was really happening and even shown visually to them. As readers or movie spectators, they almost never imagined that the cannon fire or the bayonets in hand-to-hand fighting could kill their relatives—a father, for instance, or a husband, or a brother, or the neighbor who would sometimes take such a boy to the Sunday soccer game.

Yes, I was making progress. I was learning to discriminate more sharply, think faster, judge far more cautiously. I noticed this myself and was sometimes as satisfied with myself as if I were both father and child, both teacher and pupil in one. At this time, I developed a habit I was never to lose: not to fall asleep before letting the day's events run by like a film. It was only much later that I discovered I was practicing a mnemonic device, whose effect is beginning to weaken, but not fade, only now.

In this way I also reviewed movies I had seen, newsreels as well as features. The lead performers were usually very good, well-known actors. Some were in the ensemble of the prestigious Burgtheater. One of them—his name was Alfred Gerasch—played the irresistible seducer and often the tragic hero. He was handsome; he never grimaced, even when he had to make passion or daredevil defiance credible to the audience; his gestures were youthful as well as dignified. That was how I saw him then, that is how I remember him—far more as a silent-film hero than as the stage actor whom I subsequently saw very often in the theater. Needless to say, every woman fell in love with him and, if she was married, plunged into misfortune as a result. On the other hand, many of the women whose beauty was constantly praised in the films were too old for their roles; although not ugly, they were hardly pretty, and their gestures, their pantomime, were ridiculously exaggerated, whether reflecting the pride of virtue before the fall, heartless coquetry or passionate surrender, the feigned fidelity of an adulteress or the incurable woe of abused love. Often, I indignantly left a screening at which the viewers had been asked to believe that an Alfred Gerasch would kill himself over a woman whom I would never have chosen if I had been in his shoes.

Another star of silent films was Harry Walden. He frequently played demonic men whose love could be dangerous, even deadly; these characters were seductive, their actions mysterious and contradictory. He was probably one of the first important actors I ever saw. He exerted his strongest impact by making the spectator feel almost physically how thoroughly shadow and substance can disguise one another. I had no fear of demons; I did not believe in them. But, discovering that I knew so little, that I had misunderstood so many things, grasped them inadequately, interpreted them hastily, I felt one concern: I had to understand something properly, know its true causes, ferret them out before they materialized as deeds that could be misinterpreted. In nearly all movies, evil loomed up unexpectedly, which made it all the more frightening—it had a powerful dramatic effect, which I felt even more sharply than the rest of the audience. Yet I was not moved to believe that human beings are evil. My unusual, obsessive hatred of war was partly due to the fact that soldiers had to kill each other even though they were not evil.

If I consulted archives and chronicles, I could probably obtain more precise information about those films and their actors. I could check whether and how my memory has modified my experiences at the Nestroy Kino, distorting them or even turning them upside down. However, in this case, I will leave everything to my recollections. It must be true that Harry Walden's performances and the actions of the heroes he portrayed first made me clearly recognize a problem that I have never stopped and will never stop dealing with.

Something happened that was more important than those movies, than almost everything else I experienced in those days. I registered at the local library on tiny Hafnergasse. This branch of the Central Public Library was a one-story room with long counters, behind which the librarians, two, sometimes three women, accepted and checked in the returned books and then glanced through the reserve lists. They could usually tell you right away which books were out and which were available. These volumes, nearly always bound in black, were usually in poor shape, since they reached this branch only after being worn out by the subscribers of the Central Library.

In the categories making up the reserve list, you found the letters MA or MI: Major and Minor Works. The former included fiction, plays, and poetry, and the latter everything else. You could borrow up to two titles from each category, but the librarians often added minor works, even ones that the borrower hadn't requested. And sometimes more than two.

My first reserve lists contained the titles of the most important dramatic works of the German classics. I usually received more than I had bargained for, since they gave me the thick volumes of the complete editions. I greedily wolfed down everything like a starving man. When I speak about a later phase of my life, I will try to pinpoint what these works meant to me and how they influenced me. What entranced me like a first love was the language—its richness in verse and prose, which distinguished it from everyday speech, raising it far above it, and finally the real or seeming density, since almost every sentence contained so much more than could be expected from so few words. Everything seemed to relate to everything else—the past, the future—never flat, but a mounting and falling movement, which you followed breathlessly.

As chance would have it, the first play I brought home from the library was Goethe's *Iphigenie in Tauris*. I feel as if I can still experience the strange, confusing, the uplifting and disheartening excitement aroused in me by the opening lines, spoken by Iphigenie. You have to know so much in order to understand this properly, I told myself in despair. And would I ever know enough? It was so wonderful! How awful if I were to remain incapable of reading and understanding it properly! I wouldn't give up, and I joyfully discovered that everything grew clearer from verse to verse, eventually becoming lucid, even simple, and immeasurably sad and finally full of hope.

That was exactly what I often experienced later on, when, say, a landscape shrouded in mist and fog gradually emerged, arranging itself from pieces into a meaningful whole, thus taking shape.

Four decades later, in a lovely house on the flower quay of Ile de la Cité in Paris, the aging French writer Edmond Fleg complained that he found it hard to read my novels because every chapter, every episode, began somewhere in the middle. I replied that such abruptness was characteristic of many other novels; the cinema compelled the modern novelist to parachute his readers into the middle of an unfamiliar landscape, an unforeseen situation.

But now, in discussing my first encounter with classical dramas, I realize that these early readings may have influenced the structure of my novels more strongly than the movies did. In the library editions available to borrowers, there was usually neither foreword nor afterword, practically no precise references to the setting, and only the most basic stage directions, such as "enter," "exit," or "aside." It was the plot, the action, the dialogues and monologues that always made it obvious where the action was set and what the character could see nearby and in the distance. The aspect that impressed me most deeply in 1917, at the start of my supremely important career as a borrower at the Hafnergasse library, was not so much the strange world suddenly opening up to me, as the special approach to it, which I discovered through those poetic dramas. And that inspired the words of a writer in one of my novels in 1951:

> Don't write like the regurgitators: don't supply external details, don't draw gestures or faces. Only for those for whom the essential is enough. It's time I finally stopped prostituting myself with the compliancy people expect from writers. Or else I'll give up writing.

The pale librarians, who were as undernourished as most of their customers, usually went to the cases containing the "minor works" and pulled out books that they handed to the readers together with the "major works." Chance usually played its part here. These were popular books on the problems and discoveries of the sciences, as well as famous works from all areas of knowledge. And travelogues must have excited those borrowers who could not ever look forward to going on a long trip.

The first minor works I brought home were a travel book by Gerstäcker, who was greatly esteemed; the memoirs of a noblewoman who had been a German governess at the court of a foreign prince; and finally a book by a forester about his experiences as a huntsman and as a hunting guide for princes. I read Gerstäcker and returned the other two books unread. Later I happened to receive *Gulliver's Travels* and Nietzsche's *Thus Spake Zarathustra* together, as well as other major works, of course, which, as I have said, were classical dramas for many weeks on end.

The influence of Swift must be the same on all young people. It was only later that I realized these stories are anything but cheerful and that the humor of the opening chapters inadequately conceals the hatred, which always keeps surfacing later on like a pointed jet flame. Nietzsche's *Zarathustra* had the strangest effect on me. It attracted me because its diction reminded me of the language of the prophets of Israel. I knew the latter; they were mine, so to speak—and now, a German was writing as if he were one of them, yet he had come much too late. And being a Christian, he could not claim to be their descendant. As in the days when my teacher had taken me to my great-grandfather to have me recite texts and translations, I effortlessly memorized whole sentences: "What is great about man is that he is a bridge and not a purpose: what can be loved in man is that he is a transition and a downfall." The disjunction and conjunction of *Übergang* (transition) and *Untergang* (downfall) have almost become a certainty for me. One of the few I have left.

I was annoyed by what Nietzsche said about the superman and still dislike it. That was probably one of the reasons why, after just a few years, I began to condemn more and more sharply the false "solemnity," and overly yet inadequately lofty "exaltation" of this pseudo-prophetic, pseudo-biblical, and anti-biblical prose. Even when I was influenced by the revolutionary transvaluator Nietzsche, I did not stop parodying his *Zarathustra*, which provoked pious indignation now and then.

The overthrow of the czar in 1917 filled us all with such profound joy that we felt we could never express it in words. The crooked had finally been straightened again, injustice had yielded to justice—we were all convinced of that. And now, we could look forward to a speedy end to the war. But instead, the Russian armies renewed their offensive on nearly all fronts.

In May 1917, two months after the overthrow in Russia, a relatively trivial event took place. A special court of law tried the assassin Friedrich Adler and finally sentenced him to death. This two-day trial had a deep and lasting impact on thousands if not tens of thousands of young people. Despite the censorship, newspaper readers could follow the trial very closely. On the very first day, we all discovered an unusual man, the incarnation of everything that ought to be exemplary for us. Indeed, we felt we were becoming nobler and more courageous by agreeing with the detailed statements made by Friedrich Adler—in the middle of the war, unhindered by the court, in public! We were deeply moved to learn how the young scholar had prepared himself to commit this act, which, like all forms of violence, was alien to him, and thus to abandon all his personal dreams.

The important thing for him, he said, was not the *length* of his life, but the *content*. This statement, more than any Marxist doctrine and more than most revolutionary writings, influenced the decisions I was to make during my youth. In high spirits or low, in the brightness of triumphs or in the shadow of frustrations, I have always, nearly always, wanted to know: Why live? To what end? What content gives life a value that counts not only for me, not only for this or that individual? My question, at first inadequately framed, gained meaning for me in March 1917, when the Revolution won out in Russia, and in May 1917, when an individual, defying the rulers of Austria, pilloried the corruption and absurdity of war with a loud, clear voice, proclaimed every human being's right to freedom and truth, and committed his life to this right.

Friedrich Adler's sentence, as we know, was commuted to eighteen years at hard labor; but then, without his having to petition for it, he was pardoned on November 2, 1918, by Emperor Karl I, the last Hapsburg. Two years earlier, on October 21, 1916, the assassin had resigned himself to believe he would certainly not live to see his thirty-eighth year. But he did not die until 1960, at eighty-one-years old. Late in life, he resembled not only his father but also that defendant at the special court of law, who had brought a message to an entire generation, a tiding whose every word sounded like the very appeal we had been waiting for without realizing it.

The last time I saw him was several years before World War II, in a waiting room at the Paris airport. Like me, he had come to welcome Sophie Lazarsfeld, the individual psychologist from Vienna. During the hour we spent together, I kept thinking about telling him what he had meant to the boy who had been awakened at an early age. I wanted to tell him that during the trial I had not only boundlessly admired but also loved him. And that his impact had lasted for decades. But I said nothing about all that. The three of us had a good conversation, and my memories would not have fit in at all. Besides, I would have had to explain, even justify, why, despite everything, I had not followed his example, why I had not become a Social Democrat.

When I awoke this morning, roused by the monastery bells and the intense light of the June sun, I tried to take stock of what I have written about during the past few weeks. I thought of things I should have at least mentioned and other things I ought to go into more thoroughly. Well, as I have said, for a long time the certainty that I have always written only fragments in thousands of pages no longer makes me think I have failed. "It's over, there's no such thing anymore," a Berlin worker says somewhere in a book of mine. Well, there's also no such thing, of course, as writing down everything, absolutely everything. Each of us, both the reader and the author, knows the writer must select, that is, omit, toss into the giant wastebasket, anything that does not really belong to the work, because it is not important enough, not informative enough, not characteristic: strings from which no rope has been twisted, ropes that have not gotten entangled with other ropes and are now lying around, slowly rotting in the rain—still here to be condemned and yet nonexistent.

Lilienbrunngasse. That was the name of our not too short, not too narrow, not too shabby street. When I first heard the name, one hour before we left the bedbug-ridden rooming house, I felt as if my dream of Vienna were about to come true. *Lilienbrunngasse:* a well *(Brunn)*, a wellspring probably in the middle of a garden of countless lily beds. I could have written about this moment, when I believed we had finally reached the place that had drawn me for such a long time. One hour later, we were there. It was so close that we could walk. Let us waste no breath on my disappointment. What still amazes me today—more specifically since I have begun writing these memoirs—is the fact that I kept so many things from the people I lived with, whom I trusted completely. Yet I did not think I was hiding anything; I felt these matters concerned only me, as if I had to tackle everything without anyone's help. I think I already knew, as a very young psychologist, that even the most trusting, the most chatty children maintain *enclaves of secrecy*. Nevertheless, it strikes me as almost unbelievable that I did not tell my parents or my brothers about things I experienced so deeply and intensely—we cared for each other so much and felt no distrust toward each other.

And, in the waiting room of Air France, I realized I would probably never again see the old man sitting across from me. I knew precisely what I wanted to—no, had to—tell him, and yet I did not do so. Even though I usually like paying sincere compliments—not only to friends and acquaintances, but also to strangers and even adversaries.

The expression "keep it to yourself," in the sense of "keep a secret," may mean that one refuses to share knowledge or emotions with others, i.e., retreats into one's enclave. As I have already mentioned, if I was excited by a writer, painter, or performer, I would often write him a letter of thanks—but not in reality, only in my head. I have done so ever since my early youth. Sometimes though not often enough, I actually write such a letter, but only to express my agreement with or gratitude to a friend or acquaintance.

Some of the authors whose books so enthralled me back then were still alive, and some lived in Vienna. I never felt any desire to meet them during my boyhood or later on. Was it timidity, awe, an inhibiting sense of insecurity, fear of disappointing or being disappointed? Probably all those things together, but something else as well: In my home, we believed that one owed a teacher and master more gratitude and respect than the best father. At the same time, however, the most-quoted authors of chiefly religious works and commentaries were mentioned not by name but by the titles of their most important books, sometimes only by the opening words. Anecdotes were told that did not always present these learned writers in the most positive light. Their writings were praised nevertheless. Volumes that were read to pieces, falling apart, and totally useless, were burned almost worshipfully so that none of the pages would ever be dishonored by some low use.

At a very early age, I must have sensed if not suspected that an intellectual work can be more than its author and—more generally—a deed more meaningful than its doer. At the age of forty-five, I sat across from old Friedrich Adler, whose deeds (the assassination and, even more, his conduct at the special court of law) had deeply agitated me and others like me, turning us into agitators. As I gazed into his intelligent, sensitive face, I knew what we all owed him, and I also knew he was now so remote from his deeds, he and they had diverged so greatly, that there could be no bridge leading back to them.

The man sitting in front of me was a most worthy person, one of the politically most insightful men of the century; he was an assassin. To express it with more concretely: in the year 1917, after the commutation of his death sentence, one could have predicted: "In thirty years, you will no longer be an assassin."

That was not the only reason why I did not mention that past and why I did not tell him about his influence on me. Open, candid, and eloquent if not talkative since my early childhood, I have been *secretly* reticent. And my novels have broken this reticence only indirectly, in the third person. I am doing it again in these memoirs, but this time in the first person; completely aware, I dissolve these secrets for myself and the reader, and they arouse a sense of the sinister in me as often as I stumble upon them inside myself.

In the summer, when the school year was over and the admission examination for the Gymnasium was behind me, my father hired a student to coach me for the autumn examination. A few days after the tutoring began, my father made it clear to me and my teacher that I could probably manage to skip a class. My mother protested, for there were only a few weeks left, the summer was terribly hot, and I was all skin and bones—it was absurd to expect such an achievement from me. My father wouldn't give in; it never even occurred to him that I might fail.

My instructor, who spent two hours a day with me, was a friendly but unenergetic young man of moderate intelligence. Moreover, he was completely incapable of explaining a single mathematical concept or principle. It was certainly his fault that I understood things very late and inadequately at that.

During those two weeks, I was ruled by a dichotomy: I both feared and hoped that I would disappoint my father. His tendency to overestimate my abilities boundlessly would have to yield to a different estimate. I remember perfectly that Saturday morning when my father, not I, was to obtain the result of the examination. I was feverishly nervous, which astonished me. I was ambitious, of course—I knew I was, and I didn't want to suffer any failure, especially since all our friends, our countless visitors had repeatedly been told by my father that I was sure to succeed. It was wrong of him to praise me, but it was done, and the embarrassment threatened not only him but me. He would certainly not reproach me, but he would be very sad. The situation of our family had been worsening for years, ever since the start of the war. And now of all times, he would also have to lose the exaggerated hope he had pinned on me.

On that rainy September day, I ran through streets I barely knew, through residential areas that didn't interest me. I ran as if fleeing from someone and also as if strange places were a refuge from my own thoughts, readily offering the courage for indifference or the appeasing sadness of resignation. I found nothing of the sort. I had to face the music. I hurried home, taking the shortest possible route. I wanted to feign cheerfulness or at least composure, but even today I am unable to conceal any emotion. My father, who must have remained longer at synagogue, probably to help celebrate a bar mitzvah, wasn't home yet. Perhaps at that very moment, he was just getting the bad news from the secretary of the Gymnasium on Zirkusgasse. My mother acted as if she didn't notice my state of mind. She handed me a letter that had just arrived from Bobe Feygy. In Vienna I had gotten into the habit of standing at the window and gazing up at the sky. I did so now, and the view brought me calm and comfort.

Finally, I heard my father's voice and another voice, that of a perfect stranger. He had probably brought along an *orekh*, a Sabbath guest, whom he had chosen from among the more or less "bashful" beggars, the schnorrers.

"C'mon, we're going to eat now," said my mother. And as I turned around, she added, "*Narele*, little fool, how could you believe you wouldn't pass the exam?" That was how I learned I'd made it.

It was not discussed during the meal, for the schnorrer hogged the conversation. He must have considered it his professional duty to entertain his host and hostess with the story of his life. He did it with brio and caustic humor, so that we listened with great interest. He promised to honor us with another visit very soon.

The term had started ten days earlier, so I entered a classroom in which the seats and roles had already been distributed. The other pupils had known each other for over a year. A latecomer like myself is normally viewed with derisive if not distrustful curiosity, then indifference. I wore a sailor's blouse that was too small for me, short pants, and long, black socks. My shoes were wretched; one of the iron cleats was loose, banging on the floor at every step. I was given a seat in the next-to-last row on the left. It was Latin class, and the professor, who was also the homeroom teacher, was himself a refugee, for one could hear a characteristically Ruthenian accent whenever he spoke more rapidly. I didn't like the bristly hair over his severe, narrow face, which always seemed closed off.

About a week later, he called on me to translate a Latin text out loud. But then he gruffly broke in after the very first sentence, told me to come up on the podium, and ordered me to repeat the German version. I did it. He shouted, "Wrong!" and commanded me to write the sentence on the blackboard and then to read it aloud. I did so. He interrupted me again, stood up, underlined the word *"Haus"* (house) and ordered me to repeat it once again. I had to keep doing it, almost uninterruptedly, and he rebuked me each time: "Wrong!"

It turned into a game that didn't really entertain him, but seemed to fill him with inexplicable glee. The other pupils, especially those at the front desks, played along. As the skit went on, they accompanied each "Wrong!" with louder and more ingratiating laughter. The new boy, in his ridiculous sailor suit, stood helpless before them, at the mercy of the feared professor. From then on this new boy would be the class dunce.

My very first experience with a "Christian" public school had been equally grotesque. On the first day, the Polish teacher had called on the children alphabetically, and they were supposed to reply, *"Jestem"* (I'm here). When she called out "Sperber, Manès," no one answered. I looked around, astonished that there should be another Sperber in the same class. The teacher repeated the name—again to no avail, but she noticed that I kept looking around. She asked me my name. I answered, "Sperber." She said, "You dumbbell, why didn't you reply immediately?" The children, previously intimidated, burst into noisy laughter, barely catching my explanation that my first name was Munju, not Manès. That was what I was called by my family and everyone we knew. My parents had failed to inform me that the name on my birth certificate was the quite uncommon name Manès, which I had never heard. Thus for several days I, who had been considered an unusually intelligent child in the shtetl, was the class dunce, who didn't even know his own name. To punish me, the teacher had me repeat five times a day for an entire week: "I have to remember my name; My name is Sperber, Manès."

I didn't like that scrawny woman with the washed-out blond hair, and I didn't like the Poles or their language. But more important for my relationship to school in both Zablotow and Vienna was, no doubt, the fact that it always came too late, at least for me. By the time I entered the

Polish first grade, I already had almost three years of instruction behind me. I was familiar with the world and language of the Bible, and many other things as well. I could already read Hebrew and German, I knew many texts by heart, I sang songs in Yiddish, Hebrew, Aramaic, German, and Ukrainian. And naturally, I knew a lot about people, about the life of adults. How could I have been interested in this instruction in an almost foreign tongue? What could it offer me?

And now I stood on the podium, and I was being tortured by a Ukrainian. I loved his people; I also thought he knew that I was by no means stupid. As soon as the laughter of the other pupils died out, I again had to repeat the word *"Haus"* and hear the gleeful cry, "Wrong!" I didn't know what this man wanted from me, why he let half an hour go by without telling me, without correcting my mistake. Suddenly, a thought released me from the embarrassing humiliation: None of this concerns me. He's not tormenting me because he wants to teach me something, he simply enjoys humiliating a defenseless person, me. I gazed past him toward the window, at the rainy sky. I heard him and the laughter of the class, but I held my tongue. Whatever might happen, time had to grind on, the bell finally ring, announcing the end of the class.

All at once, someone grabbed my shoulders and spun me around. The professor stood in front of me, his face pale. He yelled, "Have you gone crazy? You're going to be expelled for this!" Frightened, I recoiled. Only then did I realize that my foot had tapped out the rhythm of an Aramaic Sabbath song. I raised my head, and my fear vanished, for suddenly I realized what he'd been driving at. I put one foot forward, then the second, and spoke up, shouting back into the professor's face: *"Ha-us, Ha-us!"* He slowly retreated and ominously raised his ruler, which lay on the desk—and the bell rang. The classroom was filled with a deathly hush; the laughers silently watched me get off the podium without the obligatory bow and leave the room.

I had pronounced the word *Haus* as if it were spelled *"Ho-us."* The teacher, perhaps without realizing it, had been annoyed partly because so many Slavs, including the Ruthenians, pronounce the German *au* like an *o*.

During recess, two pupils came up to me and swore that they admired my courage. I wanted to explain that I hadn't meant to provoke the teacher, and that, incredible as it might seem, I had tapped out the rhythm without realizing it. They didn't believe me, nor did the other pupils, the laughers, who timidly avoided me during the following days. I wanted to tell the two boys that I could just as readily have wept, but I didn't tell them. For after what had happened, I desperately needed to be praised and appreciated. They asked me whether I had heard of *Hashomer*, the Zionist Youth organization, *Hashomer Hatzair*, and they suggested that I join their *kvutzah* (group); their leader was a student in our Gymnasium. They met twice a week, usually on Biberstrasse, where they learned Hebrew songs, especially marches. They practiced using Morse code and reading maps, and they discussed Jewish problems, especially Palestine. On Sundays, they went on hikes in the Vienna Woods—either just their kvutzah, which consisted of fifteen boys, or with other groups, for the organization had a thousand members or even more, both boys and girls. People were serious in Hashomer (rules were strict), but they also had a lot of fun. They explained that if I wanted to, the leader of their kvutzah would come down during the second recess and invite me to the next *sikhah* (discussion). I hesitated—it was all so unexpected. Besides, I was still reeling from the scene on the podium. But they insisted and kept paying me compliments that I really didn't deserve. Once again, I didn't have the strength to say no decisively and unequivocally. Finally, I agreed. This decision was incomparably significant for me through many years and has continued to be important in many respects.

One of the first consequences was that I lost practically all interest in school. Hashomer kept taking up more and more space in our lives, partly under the effect of the events that soon kept happening faster and faster.

I did not become the class dunce. The teacher praised me in front of the other students. He especially praised me for being such a good grammarian in Latin and German, and he predicted that I would have a wonderful career as a classical philologist. During that same school year, he tried to be friendly several times in order to make me forget that initial scene. Whenever I discovered even the slightest urge within myself to forgive him or pretend to forget, I instantly suppressed it, for I scorned myself, even despised myself, at such times. That teacher, incidentally, vanished before the end of the school year; he probably returned to his homeland. I couldn't forget him, and I have never told anyone about him. But, as if obeying an ancient Jewish curse, I snuffed his name completely from my mind many years ago, and I have never tried to fish it out again.

That episode would have traumatized me had I failed to channel my despair over that undeserved, senseless humiliation into a rebellion for which I would never have consciously mustered the courage. That may explain why no one who has ever confronted me as an opponent or enemy has succeeded in humiliating me. A further, rather curious result of this experience may have been the fact that no matter what language I have learned, I have never tried to lose or even blur my foreign accent in order to sound like a native. On the contrary, I always like to make it clear that I am no native son, and that I don't have the slightest inclination to make anyone think I am or could be. Even though I know the vocabulary and characteristic expressions of several dialects and, in my novels, employ them very sparingly whenever I find it necessary, I have never attempted to speak any of them.

In fall and winter 1917, our kvutzah met in the basement of a house on Biberstrasse. The large, unheated rooms belonged to a Jewish dueling fraternity, which had set up its fencing hall here. Now its members were in the army. We fenced with their swords and sabers, imitating duelists—chiefly to keep warm. We spent most of our time learning how to speak Hebrew and studying the history of the Zionist movement and Palestinography. During our Sunday outings in the Vienna Woods, we drilled to orders in Hebrew: instructing the guard, falling into place, marching in step, and so forth. I participated very earnestly, even zealously. I was repelled by anything military, but like all the others, I understood that our goal was to escape from Diaspora life. We would never, never again, endure being not only hated, but also despised by our enemies; we would never again bow; instead, we would confront the enemy with stiff backs.

Our parents had been reluctant to leave their settlements if it wasn't necessary; they feared that in the villages they would encounter people who would irreconcilably deny them the right to exist. The leader of each of our groups that went on Sunday hikes carried a blue-and-white flag showing the Star of David. It was agreed that we would not let any insult or challenge go unanswered, unpunished. Even if we were weaker and less numerous than our attackers, we would have to stand our ground. Carry our heads high, look everyone in the eye, never shrink from conflict and battle, never, never again run away! Hashomer taught us that as well as the virtues encouraged by the German youth movement: honesty, truthfulness, helpfulness, and a good deed every day. "Be prepared!" But before the year 1918 ended, Hashomer changed from a

Jewish scouting organization to a free and essentially revolutionary youth movement. This change was first prompted, no doubt, by the oldest among us, young men on furlough from the front lines who told us what they were experiencing there. The Russian Revolution nurtured our interest in the Social Revolutionaries, the descendants of the Narodniki, and in the anarcho-communist theory of Kropotkin, the revolutionary prince, far more than in Marxism. Kropotkin's memoirs and his *Mutual Aid* made a deep impact on us and certainly helped convince the Vienna Hashomer of the ideas and goals that were subsequently realized in the kibbutz.

For us, everything was connected: the almost militaristic posture during physical exercise, five-mile hikes, and the use of army terminology; the utterly free, endless discussions in which we talked ourselves hoarse, liberating ourselves from all pressures; the growing hostility toward war, toward anyone who profited from it, toward all bourgeois life and all authoritarianism; the martial marching songs and the melancholy Yiddish folk songs, the revolutionary songs of the Jewish and gentile labor movement and the *nigunim*, the melodies crooned in the Hasidic homes and synagogues.

The members of Hashomer, almost all of them high-school and university students, came from bourgeois or petty-bourgeois families who had fled to Vienna from Galicia or Bukovina. Their social status could have led them to a certain kind of assimilation, a gradual estrangement from Judaism, from its faith and customs. But here, the organization reached into the lives of these young people and their families in an astonishingly contradictory way. The conscious or unconscious tendency toward assimilation left room for a firm desire to be actively Jewish. At the same time, the younger generation alienated itself from their elders, openly attacking their traditional way of life and thereby them. The generation gap that threatens immigrant families everywhere was made almost inevitable by Hashomer and remained generally incomprehensible to our parents. They had feared that their children might move away from Judaism and thus from them. This alienation came about, not because the children assimilated, but because they wished to be different from their mothers and fathers. The parents, who could not help feeling that their children almost scornfully rejected their Galut Judaism, were terribly hurt. But the children seemed quite indifferent. *Seemed,* for most of my comrades probably went through what I did: I had found a *we* in the movement, a *we* that I had been urgently seeking since the winter of

1915. In those days I could not anticipate that I would feel part of a community that would loosen and finally destroy my attachment to my family—without terminating my emotional tie to my parents. One reason was not only the gap between the generations and the natural process of their growing apart, but mainly the fact that we boys, in order to find ourselves in the midst of an urban, cosmopolitan civilization, wanted to retain certain things from the shtetl, but not belong to it anymore. That was the start of a crisis that had thoroughly churning, partially destructive effect, the full scope of which, I believe, no one sensed.

In the winter of 1917–18 the population of Vienna finally realized that their complaints about hunger and all kinds of shortages had been valid but exaggerated. Now life became harder by the day. Sometimes you could almost hear the big city struggling arduously for its breath, like a critically ill patient.

Badly dressed, inadequately protected against cold and wet, people had had to spend hours upon hours outdoors: lining up in the morning and at all times of the day, of course. But now, the lines often formed before morning and, eventually, in the middle of the night. Everyone wanted to be at least relatively certain that there would still be something left when it was his turn to buy. For it often happened that after a night of waiting, the "Sold-out" sign would be put up just as you finally managed to reach the threshold of the shop. Yes, the populace of Vienna—women, men, old people, children—waited all through the long hours of windy, frosty, rainy nights in poorly lit or unlit streets, hoping to grab a kilogram of potatoes, which were often frozen and almost inedible. This is the end; it can't get any worse, the people on line comforted one another. But as things turned out, it *could* get worse.

Much as our parents wanted to avoid it, it finally became absolutely necessary for us children to stand in line too. At this point, everything that had disappointed me about Vienna in summer 1916 became unimportant. Around me was not imperial magnificence but universal suffering, altering faces so deeply that they sometimes looked alike even when viewed up close. This happened because the *naked humanity* that marks a famished face can appear in only a few, barely differentiated forms.

I was not yet familiar with Expressionist art and would probably not have understood the term. I hadn't yet seen Egon Schiele's paintings or the works of the Cubists. When I stumbled upon them, some two years later, I recognized the warped, twisted faces of people with whom I had lined up before daybreak or in the gray hours of dawn, both resigned and indignant, frequently soaked and frozen, waiting for the shopkeeper to start selling at last, hoping I could get into his store before everything was gone.

I have very frequently thought back to the starving, freezing, humiliated city of Vienna—with deep compassion, but also with astonishment and admiration. There were many concerts in those days. I didn't attend them, but I read the posters carefully. The theaters usually played to sold-out houses. Lectures and readings were well attended every evening, though the auditoriums were heated insufficiently or not at all. A few minutes from my street, behind the Commodities Exchange on Taborstrasse, a Jewish welfare organization, headed by an extremely active, relatively young woman named Anita Müller, had set up a place to drink tea and warm up. It was always crowded until closing time. The patrons were old people, childless wives of soldiers, furloughed military men whose families lived in enemy-occupied territories, war invalids, and professional schnorrers.

Thanks to the public library, I had enough books. The more I read, the more unbridled my reading lust became. Every book pointed to so many others, teaching me how little I knew, telling me I had a rendezvous with hundreds, thousands of writers, with countless works. However, all these books—aside from the usually mindless, ridiculously exaggerated patriotic war books—came from the prewar period. The tiny evening gazette, my cheap daily newspaper, did not suffice. Dozens of dailies and weeklies lay around in the coffee houses, but I couldn't afford to go because I had meanwhile left my job distributing silverware. Besides, it was out of the question for me to visit a café, because boys my age were not really welcome without an adult.

I frequented the "hall"—I think that was the name of the tea room—every evening, for there were a lot of newspapers here, though they weren't intact, after passing through so many hands. The staff and the philanthropic helpers tried to keep the noise down and maintain order and cleanliness, but their efforts were futile. I was used to reading without being bothered by conversations that kept bombarding my ears.

In this hall I encountered a man who changed his name often, as if to escape detection. But since everyone knew it was he bearing the new name, the whole thing was a game that amused chiefly him, to be sure, but the others as well.

I was reaching for a newspaper I had spotted on a chair when someone grabbed my arm from behind. I turned and saw a sickly man with the emaciated face of a starveling. He wore a uniform without insignia and, though the hall was very warm, a gray fur cap on his head. His right sleeve hung down empty; he must have been a war invalid. Yanking the newspaper from my hand, he shouted in a nasty tone of voice, "First me, then you!" I gazed at him, speechless, embarrassed, for I didn't know whether it was cowardly to give in or improper to fight over a newspaper with a sick man, since I could just as easily read it after him. My embarrassment grew when he suddenly burst into wild laughter, which drew two young soldiers in shabby uniforms. They stationed themselves next to him. After peering at me curiously, they laughed in my face like sycophantic pupils flattering a teacher who is trying to be funny. At a sign from the one-armed man, they promptly fell silent. With an elegant gesture, he asked me to join him at his table, where his two buddies also sat down. He said:

"I am First Lieutenant Grimme. Perhaps I'm not a first lieutenant. And besides, it's no one's business whether my name is Grimme or something else. Izzat clear? Good. And what's your name? Who are you? Why do you come here every evening? Don't you have any family, or are you a vagabond, a vagrant?"

For a moment, I wondered whether I should answer, and then I answered in great detail because I felt that this man was of concern to me, and I wanted to find out why. I was not surprised that he was interested in me, for more and more adults would start conversations with me. And, as I have already said, I liked and still like to talk. When I was finished, he pointed to the newspaper and said, "So, if you're already a politician, so to speak, tell me quickly: Who is this Kerensky, what's he after? And who is Martov, say? And who is Trotsky and who is Lenin? What are these guys after, anyway? And you, who are you for?"

He listened to my answer, more and more impatiently, finally breaking in to exclaim, "Good. You know and you don't know. Or else you know, but don't understand. Or else you understand, but you really misunderstand—like these two jerks here, who won't leave me alone. The two of them are so stupid that they're actually happy in this world. This guy next to me is Yankel, but he's grateful if you call him Ulrich. He's also got delusions of grandeur; he claims he was a sergeant. The other guy, his name's Chaskel, he'd be a Spinoza if he were as smart as he's good. Okay, now take this lousy newspaper and go sit somewhere else. Tomorrow or the day after, I'll explain who's who and what's what."

I quickly stood up, wanted to shake hands but hesitated, for it might be unpleasant for him. Instead, I merely smiled at him. He bared his head and waved his fur cap at me, exaggerating ironically. Ulrich and Chaskel guffawed loudly again.

I looked forward to our next meeting with great curiosity, but it proved disappointing. Grimme was a changed man. He spoke uninterruptedly, and I understood little of what he so eagerly rattled off, at times with what seemed like unwarranted vehemence. His words were unarticulated, squeezed out of his half-open mouth. They virtually dangled from his quivering lips, like mucus, before he finally spat them out, immensely annoyed with himself.

Eventually, I got used to him and listened patiently, especially after Chaskel explained this odd, very frequent change: the first lieutenant couldn't stand his dentures; they irritated his gums, causing swellings and chafings. "Without his false teeth, he doesn't feel right, but he can talk like a human being. And with them, he feels awful," said Chaskel. "Poor Herr Krakowiak! His right arm's gone, his teeth are gone, and his heart and lungs aren't what they oughta be!"

During our first few conversations, Grimme-Krakowiak informed me that he was actively preparing the revolution—not he alone, of course, but there weren't many who knew as precisely as he: first, what absolutely had to be done, and second, what absolutely had to be prevented. He cited names I didn't know, but which cropped up in the thin pamphlets he lent me. I couldn't keep them; I had to "get them under my belt" then and there, as he put it, in a German that was impeccable but quite bizarre, because the level of the vocabulary kept changing, sometimes in the middle of a sentence. First he spoke like a worker, preferably one of those Viennese Czechs, whose accents were mimicked by their native-born neighbors, often derisively, sometimes with baiting sarcasm. Then he would switch into a frequently pompous, literary German, particularly when he explained that there was only one way to free humanity: the revolution, which would leave not a stone standing. Its goal: *ungoverned socialism*, the implementation of the strictest, that is, most humane, anarchistic program. Grimme's hollow—no, haggard—cheeks turned red when he spoke those words—whenever he pronounced the phrase "ungoverned Socialism" with his dentures in his mouth, it sounded like the title of a love poem.

Without meaning to, I caused the first of many crises in our relationship. I mentioned Trotsky, quoting a line from him in a newspaper, and said that he and Lenin would put a speedy end to the war. Grimme broke in: "You're just parroting newspaper garbage. You're getting stupider every day." He talked a blue streak; his vehemence became bound-less. All at once, he yanked the false teeth from his mouth and fell silent. I left the table, but Ulrich quickly caught up with me, saying that the Herr First Lieutenant couldn't stand the sight of me because I was a fool and a hypocrite like all Marxists. At the time, I knew Marx only from constantly reprinted quotations. I didn't know for sure what a Marxist was, and I didn't believe I was one myself. I was against war; I advocated equal rights for all human beings, especially Jews, who were denied equal rights in most countries. I favored a Jewish homeland in Palestine, as Lord Balfour had promised the Jews just a few weeks earlier. Since Kerensky was prolonging the war even after the overthrow of the czar, he was an enemy. Since Lenin and Trotsky wanted to conclude peace right away, the victory of their revolution meant something good for all the nations once ruled by the czar, and for all poor people, especially the peasants. I believed these things as so many others did.

Some two weeks later, Chaskel came to my corner, interrupted my reading, and asked me to come back to Krakowiak immediately. I replied that I would probably do it some day, but not now, not under orders.

"What do you mean, not now?" asked Chaskel, a burly country Jew, on whom everything—his face, his shoulders, his hands—was much too broad. He gaped as if I had suddenly become unrecognizable. He sat down next to me and began to tighten his puttees, which always seemed to be rolling down, ready to fall apart. Meanwhile he murmured, almost in a soliloquy: "When an officer says, 'Come,' you come. What's wrong, what did he do to you? Did he spit in your soup? Herr Krakowiak is offended, he spits blood out of his lungs, and then a boy comes along and wants to annoy him even more." I pretended I wasn't listening, and kept reading. He stood up at last, looked around thoughtfully, and heaved a loud sigh. Suddenly, he threw his arms around my hips. I struggled; everyone stared at us—this Jewish peasant in uniform and me, whom he half-carried, half-pushed all the way to Grimme's table. Chaskel gently placed me on a chair. The noise in the hall had died out. All eyes were on us—on me, the kidnap victim, so to speak; on the one-armed man, whom the others had long since found sinister; and on Chaskel, who stook there with his arms spread as if he were about to grab me again. I wanted to protest, but I had to laugh. The laughter quickly spread, filling the entire room, and lasting for a long time. I had tears in my eyes from laughing so hard, but probably also because of the violence that had just been done to me.

Grimme's laughter, which sounded like wild barking, was interrupted by a coughing fit. When he finally caught his breath again, he signaled me to calm down. He said, "Wipe your eyes and read!" He handed me a Yiddish journal (written in the Hebrew alphabet). Noticing that I wasn't used to reading Yiddish, he explained that this was a monthly periodical, which came from America rather circuitously. His hints didn't make it clear whether the publishers were Anarchists or left-wing Social Revolutionaries. What he read to me were sentences he had underlined in an article on Trotsky, who was shown in a photo taken in 1903. The then twenty-five-year-old did not look very much like the leader of the victorious revolution, or his pictures, which were published almost daily in newspapers.

I listened closely, for it was interesting. Everyone was talking about Trotsky, but only now did I learn who the man really was. The author of that long article had been a member of Trotsky's St. Petersburg Soviets in 1905 and had spent a lot of time with him later on, in America. What Grimme stressed most were the writer's arguments against Trotsky and Marxism, against both the Menshiviks and the Bolsheviks. I did not grasp everything, especially the reference to all sorts of congresses and conflicts; most of the names were meaningless for me. Though I was a bookworm, I had never read a political book. Thus Grimme was right, I realized now; I knew nothing, I understood little, and I misunderstood many things. For what that author had written in September 1917 boiled down to the conclusion that Trotsky, Lenin, and all their sort would not liberate anyone if they were victorious—not the proletariat, not the peasantry, and not the nations suppressed by the czar. Instead, they would establish a dictatorship in the name of the revolution, a new despotism. That sounded incredible to me, I told Grimme, unbelievable, a vicious slander. I infuriated him, of course, but he controlled himself and gave me a long speech. He didn't succeed in convincing me; I barely listened and only wanted to get away from him as quickly as possible. He didn't seem to notice and kept talking on and on. Finally, it became late, and besides, I said to him, the point wasn't really to convince me.

"You're wrong. I believe in individuals. For each person is an individual," said Grimme, rebuking me.

"I don't understand," I broke in and stood up. "The revolutions in March and November were both fought by the masses."

"So join the masses!" Grimme shouted. "And don't show your face around here again. Go to hell!"

I left him and his grotesque retinue. I was sad that things between us had to end like that, and yet I was glad it was over. I knew his confused opinions now and I didn't know what to do with them. The ideas he kept so vehemently presenting contradicted everything I was looking for in Hashomer and found at almost every meeting; a sense of belonging and freedom. We all believed that the people—of every nation—contained great virtues, creative energy, and that the new era belonged to the people: the new era was approaching inexorably.

There was another reason why I was happy about that break. That impatient man bothered me because he always seemed to be expecting something from me—I couldn't quite tell what. To agree with him about everything? Probably. Even if I had wanted to pretend I did, I couldn't have pulled it off, and he would have seen through me. Besides, I sensed quite clearly that he wasn't so much concerned about me, that he didn't care about me one way or the other. He believed he had very little time left, and so I was the future witness for him, as it were. I know that now, for I have quite often met old men who were seeking their future witnesses. Indeed, sometimes, I myself must resist the temptation of speaking to a young man as if he were the harbinger of posterity. And even when I was no longer young, well-known, indeed, famous men, while conversing with me, have presented the elements of an obituary or a biographical essay, hoping I would make good use of the material at the proper time.

In winter 1917–18, however, I was only twelve years old. What could that sick man expect of me? Well, he knew I was in Hashomer, and perhaps hoped I would influence my comrades with his ideas. He believed in the harvest. A man had only to sow. I was supposed to scatter his seed.

He had remained alien to me, for I had failed to learn from him where he came from, what his real name was, where his family lived. All I knew was his age: thirty-two. Ulrich spoke about him admiringly and cunningly, that is, diminishing him by using a "recoil effect," so to speak. He claimed that Grimme's name was Yonas, and that he came from a rich family in Cracow. He had fought with his widowed mother and his sister and refused to accept even a penny from them. But Ulrich and Chaskel provided the first lieutenant with money from his mother. "And do you know what I'm about to tell you? Our Pan Yonas-Krakowiak-Grimme-Leszczinsky knows it damn well. He takes the money, but he wants us to be stupid enough not to notice that he knows everything." Another time, the bogus Ulrich explained to me that Chaskel and he stuck by the first lieutenant because he had managed to get the two of them out of the army.

Whatever I thus learned was meager, imprecise, and vague. But at this point, I didn't want to know anymore, for I stayed away from the warm tea room, from the old people, the schnorrers, and Grimme. Hashomer absorbed me more and more, even early in the evening. In the late evening, I had to help at home. We filled cigarettes. An agile young man brought the tobacco and the wrappers, which we were supposed to stuff sparingly, according to his directions. Where he got his tobacco from was his secret, he often repeated proudly. This home labor was not paid too badly. Furthermore, we all pitched in, except for my youngest brother, and sometimes we were helped by our visitors, who were as numerous as ever, though many refugees had returned home to the liberated territories. School didn't use up more than half my day, for I did my homework during recess. In classes I would read whenever possible, always keeping a book on or under my desk. We comrades of Hashomer had a lot to say to one another and occasionally passed notes in class. Sometimes the professors caught us and read our notes, shaking their heads, for they couldn't understand the allusive texts. The smarter teachers soon noticed that their reproaches had no effect on us, and they left us in peace. In the preface to my essay collection *The Heel of Achilles*, I described a scene that took place during the first few months of 1918. I was called on in school to tell everything I knew about the hero Achilles, and I replied:

> "Achilles was not a real warrior and not a hero, for his almost complete invincibility made him incapable of being courageous or cowardly. He had no right to participate in the battles of men who could be wounded so easily!"
>
> The teacher gazed at the scorner of Achilles—a poorly dressed, undernourished boy, a victim of the shortages and profiteers, a twelve-year-old who had already fallen prey to rebellious ideas.

The claim to authority embodied by the teacher, by adults in general, did not change. But only the most stupid and backward among them could fail to notice that the belief in the legitimacy of their claim was shrinking visibly. Pupils were often yelled at, had to do extra homework as punishment, or stay after school. But these strokes all missed. The knives had become so dull that the steel blades seemed to have changed into rotten wood.

I was by no means insolent. But I was used to looking every person in the eye, even eager to do so. And it must have been my only seemingly melancholy haughtiness that may at times have appeared like defiance.

Yet I didn't want to defy anyone—not my teachers and certainly not First Lieutenant Grimme. Still, if I felt something to be true, I might conceal it, but I couldn't distort or deny it. That was one reason I didn't want to meet Grimme anymore. Also, at Hashomer I had the possibility of speaking my mind and I discovered the happiness of friendship, which became more and more important to me over the decades.

At that time, an incident occurred at a Viennese theater. It was thoroughly discussed in the newspapers and also in our home as we filled cigarettes. During a performance, we were told, a young soldier on furlough had taken a shot at an actor, who, as an examining magistrate, was questioning a young man, intelligently, but insidiously. It was a dramatic version of Dostoyevski's *Crime and Punishment*. I had read many stories by Maxim Gorky, Tolstoy's *Cossacks*, and tales by Gogol. But it was only after this incident that I read Dostoyevski's novel. Later on in a biographical essay I tried to explain its effect, as well as that of his other works:

> I realized that anything belonging to Dostoyevski's fictitious world, which was so remote in space and time, concerned me, as if I had blundered into it unexpectedly and could never find the road back. Today, half a century later, his fiction maintains that same, urgent level of reality. One does not confront his work, one is involved in it, swept into it—as though we were watching a painting—a landscape, say,—and were suddenly carried off by some unsuspected force from our own space into the painted space. Anyone reading Dostoyevsky as he intended to be read . . . becomes a participant, and is drawn in so profoundly that he turns into an accomplice, a culprit as if by some evil spell.

Obviously, my encounter with Rodion Raskolnikov was one of the most important events of my early adolescence. I was thirteen. Whatever his age, no attentive reader can escape the overwhelming impact made by young Rodio through both his unbelievable deed and—almost more penetrating, more tormenting—the seemingly relentless logic of his confusion. Everything he looked for, said, did, or did not do was of profound interest to me, but I didn't like him, and I despised the treacherous murder he committed. This novel provided me with a permanent warning against one of our most dangerous temptations: the *false alternative*. Nevertheless, I did yield to this temptation once, in politics. It happened during several extremely difficult years, when it seemed almost impossible to reject the false alternative forced upon us by both sides.

It was under Dostoyevski's influence that I first weighed the possibility of becoming a writer, a novelist. No, I didn't want to emulate him, or write like him, or invent Raskolnikovs or humiliated drunkards or innocent whores. Just what did I want? I didn't know, and the question didn't haunt me. I thought about the future often enough, but only as a person belonging to a *we*; the future would belong to us, not *just* me, but *also* me.

At the end of our street, very close to the Marienbrücke, there was a soup kitchen, which had been set up by a cooperative in a basement. It was somewhat better than the Jewish one I had worked in. It wasn't as shabby, it was more like one of those meeting rooms in second-class hotels, which were rented for lectures, concerts, and large family celebrations. Since there was less and less to eat, the cooperative rented the space out almost every evening. I could usually get in without a ticket. I was young, looked penniless, and always sat in a back row—not out of modesty, but because it was easier to slip out when the performances were boring or I had to get home earlier. (My family sincerely appreciated my cigarette-stuffing. It was probably the only manual work I could do in an above-average way.)

It was in this basement that I was to see the first lieutenant again, much to my surprise, some two months after our break. The gathering was legal, that is, permitted by the police. But it was secretly political. The announced title was *The World of Tomorrow*. Naturally, a police agent was present, but he did not sit on the platform as was normal during political functions. The room was almost full; the audience was made up of both regular visitors and newcomers. A slender woman in black appeared on the podium. At first, her voice was barely audible. But this changed very quickly, when she suddenly spoke as if confronting violent aggression. For half an hour, more and more vehemently, she kept repeating a statement that she claimed was proven: Human beings wage wars only because they eat meat—that was the only reason. And that was the cause of our misery. Anyone who wanted peace had to start with himself and become a vegetarian. Vegetarians were peaceful people. They couldn't be anything but benevolent and peace-loving.

The next speaker was a man with black glasses, a war invalid. He both started and concluded his brief talk with the cry, "Never again war!"

The audience repeated these words; an old lady led the blind man back to his seat. Then came the musical interlude, which had been announced in great detail. An astonishingly well-nourished violinist, unaccompanied, played revolutionary songs, which were received with great applause. The no longer young, bearded man who then took the floor was obviously a practiced speaker from the very start. "Our topic is the world of tomorrow," he said by way of introduction. "This world has already begun. Today is already tomorrow. Not here, of course, but in St. Petersburg and Moscow." There were shouts of "Bravo! Long live Trotsky!" The speaker received the applause, nodding his head. He was sure of his cause and also of his friends, who were well distributed throughout the room. Whenever he ended a sentence on a fortissimo, they clapped. He thrust his hand into his trouser pocket and tossed back his head—like Lenin, who had been shown in that pose by a newspaper photo.

Shortly after that came the completely unexpected incident. No sooner had the speaker announced loudly, "The freedom of tomorrow, true freedom, exists where the Soviets rule today," than we heard the wild scream: "Lies! Lies! Insolent masquerade!" Grimme suddenly stood there, shaking his fist at the speaker and shouting, "It's not the councils that rule there, but a Bolshevik clique, they've robbed the workers' and soldiers' councils of power and broken up the constituent assembly with bayonets!" The words came tumbling out; only a few individual ones were clear. But you felt that the one-armed man was discharging a long-pent-up fury, and that he knew what he was talking about. Jumping up in my corner, I stared at him. He stood there in the light of a powerful ceiling lamp, his forehead sweaty under his dark hair, his eyes glowing, his lips trembling. This was the first time I'd seen him in a suit. His mufti looked like a disguise. He was obviously straining very hard to control his voice, but he couldn't manage. When he was interrupted by many shouts, reviled as a counterrevolutionary, an egotist, an anarchistic loudmouth, and finally a paid provocateur, he lost control entirely—his words were no longer intelligible. A few people laughed. I couldn't stand it and quickly left the place. There was no way to help him. Yet I knew how offended he'd be when he discovered I had witnessed his defeat.

That night I couldn't sleep. It was the first time I couldn't take refuge in a book, because I was obsessively haunted by the thought of someone who had remained basically foreign to me: the thought of that high-handed "individual," that critically ill, one-armed man, who knew everything better, and had two ignoramuses confirm it all the time, who carried on about "ungoverned Socialism," which would transform everything, conquer grief and death.

I was moved so deeply, not by pity, which I felt painfully, but because the situation of an individual persecuted by a mob aroused that always unpleasant memory of the young madman who had been stoned by boys, including myself. This time I was innocent. But should I have dashed to Grimme's aid? Yet what could I have accomplished—a boy against adults clustering around a politician, a thoroughly practiced speaker? Nothing. I could have done absolutely nothing for him. And besides, he had disrupted the speech with insulting words, heckling not only the speaker but also the audience. Finally, I had avoided the tea room for some time now because I didn't agree with him and couldn't bear associating with him. All this was true, I thought to myself, but perhaps I had remained silent and then sneaked out because I lacked the courage to heckle even once in favor of the anarchist, who had attacked on all sides. Had fear— that is, cowardice—kept me from showing even the least sign of solidarity with the critically ill, completely isolated man? If he learned I had witnessed the incident would he be offended? Probably. But wouldn't it have been much more important to wait at the exit and walk him home?

That sleepless night has remained so vivid in my mind because it was the first time I ever distrustfully questioned my own motives. I did not and do not have any urge for self-torment; brooding, especially while in a bad mood, is completely alien to me.

But I went around in circles because I failed to realize that my questioning was honest but vain. I didn't know that self-accusations conceal justification, vindication, and tacit self-praise. Certainly, my self-doubt was sincere. But behind it and my reproaches against myself, which I promptly invalidated, was the vanity that strengthens the self-esteem of the accused when he can be his own judge.

At that time, spring 1918, our youth organization was changing more rapidly—not on the outside, for we were still marching in rank and file along the highways; we still enjoyed the forest and meadow games of the boyscouts. But those were only remnants, so to speak, for we were convinced that everything would have to change. Little by little, even the youngest in the movement took it for granted that we now had to determine precisely how to transform education into self-education and to develop a *youth culture*, a *new youth-person*. This dream of everlasting spring came to us from the German youth movement, from the oath that young people had sworn on the Hoher Meissner to lead lives of inner truthfulness. Our rejection of society, of the authoritarian school, and middle-class, petit-bourgeois people was also fed by Wyneken's juvenism, which made us believe that youth was not just a transitional biological phase but could generate fundamentally new values and eventually overcome the bourgeois adult culture.

Strange how everything met, flowed together, and became harmonious. We enriched our treasury of songs with the *Zupfgeigenhansel*, and sang so many different things with equal joy: the old German military marches, Hasidic *nigunim*, German canons, and the revolutionary songs from Russia. We daydreamed about the rejuvenated Jewish nation that would create a new society in Palestine after draining the swamps, removing the stones and rocks, and reclaiming the soil. We could not gauge how much of this was wishful thinking, anticipation, or a grand plan that could be carried out. In the middle of the tremendous misery of war, which each of us felt personally, we were inspired by hopes that promised to push our everyday lives into the past. I nurtured, even shaped these hopes very intensely, no doubt because they fit in with my peculiar habit of fictitiously removing the present. For many youngsters like me, Hashomer became a never-waning wellspring of active happiness that both made demands and helped us along. And it remained that way for several years.

We met every day during summer vacation, no longer in the usually unlit taverns, but on the shores of the Danube and the Danube Canal and in the meadows of the Prater. We rented dinghies and paddle boats and spent hours on the water. We went to soccer games together, especially those of Hakoah, the Jewish athletic club. We played soccer and handball ourselves. We spent days and nights in the Vienna Woods, which we loved even though they were disfigured by trenches, and their groves and meadows were filthy and neglected.

The fruit trees were thriving that year; we could eat our fill in summer and early fall of 1918. People had hoped for grain deliveries from the Ukraine after the "Bread Peace" of Brest-Litovsk; but these hopes did not materialize. Everyone knew we were facing a terrible winter. At the beginning of the year, workers in factories vital to the war effort had gone on strike, protesting the curtailment of the already meager bread rations. People spoke of pacifist gatherings, which took place more and more often—with or without permits.

During vacation I had time to read a lot more than usual. Since the "minor works" the librarians had thrust at me were almost never political, my political knowledge remained on the level of an uninformed newspaper reader. Max Stirner was one of the names that Grimme mentioned quite often. When he spoke about *The Individual,* he was referring to Stirner's *The Individual and His Property.* I located this book in the library, but read only the first few pages. One sentence impressed me: "I placed my thing on nothing, I placed my thing on myself." However, I soon realized that this variant of a verse by Goethe was funny but unclear, perhaps even pointless. I was certainly doing Stirner an injustice, for I didn't understand him. And when I really read him, several years later, I found rather interesting remarks but was still disappointed. Quite a few works are often cited but very seldom read; now and then, someone makes such a book his bible. I have no idea why Grimme felt that Max Stirner offered him the gospel of individual freedom and definitive, all-encompassing social emancipation. He had read *The Individual* in the trenches, under steady fire from the enemy artillery, he once told me, as if that explained everything.

For Jews the end of summer is marked by the New Year's Feast, Rosh Hashanah, and the Day of Atonement, Yom Kippur. During the weeks of September 1918, my parents and I, as always, went to the *shul* set up by West Galician refugees in a floor-through apartment. Most of them were known as Beltzers; that is, they were followers of the dynasty of the Rabbi of Beltz, a dynasty regarded as extremely fanatical and politically reactionary, unconditionally loyal to the government, and anti-Zionist. For us, these Hasidim were "wild" worshipers. They gesticulated indefatigably, rocking their upper bodies and twisting their heads to the right and the left. They never sang, and they barely psalmodized. Instead, they shouted their prayers as if hurling them into the face of the Reboyne shel Oylem, Master of the Universe. These violent services impressed me with their boundless intensity, but I disliked them because I was used to scanned recitations and to melodies that usually aroused a feeling of melancholy tenderness.

My neighbors' screams were disconcerting, and their gestures annoyed me. I barely opened my mouth; I read a page or two of the prayer book to myself. They didn't even arouse the malaise that their fulsome praise had triggered in me several years earlier, in the shtetl. At that time I had asked myself whether God was really so insatiably greedy for obsequiousness. And now I peered around and saw my father, almost entirely shrouded in his prayer shawl. In the thick of that din, I listened to his soft voice chanting the psalm, *"Min hametsar karati. . . ."* (from the depths I called. . .). A sharp pain shot through me, for now I was certain: God does not exist, he never existed, he will never exist. I wasn't upset by this thought, yet I didn't feel liberated—I didn't feel as if I had thrown off a burden. Rather, I felt sorry for myself, for I knew I would be unable to conceal my lack of faith, and I would disappoint my father terribly—even endanger, perhaps destroy our relationship.

I feel as if I can remember every day of the autumn of 1918. I can't, of course, but many details surface, minor and significant events, most of which remain fragmentary, as if each were almost swallowed up by the subsequent ones. Events passed more swiftly every day, and we got used to it anew every day. Impossible, possible, probable—everything at once; anything was interchangeable and could be mistaken for anything else.

That summer I had distanced myself from politics. To be sure, we were for the Russian Revolution, even though it was not yet fulfilling its promise. We were against continuing the war; we favored ending it without forced contributions or annexations. We were against profiteers, against capitalists, against everyone who gained from the misery. But it was summer, and we youngsters were happy. Now, however, the autumn returned, the fifth autumn of war. The worst cannot get worse? It became unbearable—the violence had to be terminated violently. I ran to meetings where the speakers, mostly oppositional Socialists, demanded an immediate end to the war without any further delay. They spoke breathlessly; the police commissioner, who sat next to the organizers of the meeting, could interfere at any moment, order them to stop talking, or even have the room cleared. . . .

And things soon reached that pass. We found ourselves outdoors again, on the dark street, in cold rains, pushed away and finally driven apart by the police. We quickly began to sing the "Internationale" and the song of the Russian revolutionaries of 1905: "Brothers, to the sun, to freedom!" And we repeated the slogans. Then, I usually walked the blind war invalid back to the outer district, to the house in which he had found a bed, but no room to spend his days in.

In late October I ran into Grimme at a meeting. He wore a field-gray windbreaker and cavalry trousers with leather puttees. His face was changed. He didn't look better, but the torment had vanished from his mouth. He smiled at me—the first time since we had met—and said: "This and the other, everything is getting better and will get a lot better still. You've probably noticed I have good dentures now. They don't chafe my gums anymore, I can talk as much as I like. And everything is moving, no stone will be left standing. You'll see."

I was amazed to realize that I was very glad to see him. "I never saw you smile before," he said. "Now all at once you can smile, precisely because now everything's possible. Did you notice, for instance, that the commissioner didn't let out a peep when the entire auditorium applauded the idea of attacking the police?"

Together, we walked the blind man home. On the way back, I asked Grimme about his satellites. "They're decent guys, reliable guards," he replied; he also informed me that there was a Red Guard, a mixture of various elements, good ones and not so good ones, mainly soldiers on leave, especially men who had demobilized themselves.

"If you were sixteen, we could take you in, but—when were you born?" he asked.

"I was born on December 12, 1905."

He regretted that I was much too young and too weak, but he consoled me with the promise that he would find some use for me. Despite all our conflicts, he still regarded me as his supporter. By now, that was far less astonishing than it might have been earlier. Quite a few people would accept a man's opinion in the evening, then reject it in the morning, calling it completely stupid or criminal, maybe even reporting the man to the police. Our class teachers, mostly petit-bourgeois philistines who took every opportunity to stress their loyalty to the hereditary imperial house, now hesitantly voiced their anxiety about the disorder that could be caused, especially by deserters, with whom the city was teeming. But these teachers forgot to mention the kaiser or the army, which had to obey the commander-in-chief unconditionally.

Taking his leave, Grimme said he was counting on me and handed me a note on which his address was printed with a rubber stamp. He hurried back and whispered, "It's my staff chancelry, someone's there all the time, day or night. Chaskel or Ulrich or someone else, a reliable Red Guard. Simply ask for Comrade Langer, that's my name now."

We seldom had visitors in our apartment, for my father wasn't in Vienna, he was in Zablotow, trying to save whatever could be saved of his property. He wasn't getting anywhere, which was why he kept putting off his return. We were worried about him; I spent many hours, even days, in the unheated waiting rooms or on the windy platforms of North Station, until he finally arrived after a hazardous trip through the collapsing empire. The cars of his train were painted with Czech slogans and the first line of the Czech anthem, *Kde domov můj*.

He was surprised that the Austrian kaiser hadn't yet abdicated and that the republic hadn't been proclaimed. He took it for granted that all this would come about—it was as obvious as the fact that day followed night. Just two years earlier, he had wept for the deceased emperor. But now for my father, as for almost everyone else, the very recent past had vanished into an unreachable distance. Anxieties about the coming day overshadowed everything that had ever happened. My father told us about the Polish legioneers who wanted to secure East Galicia for the new Poland, and about the Ruthenians, who wanted to set up their own West Ukrainian republic. The conflict could lead to bloody fighting. And thus the Jews, who formed the majority in the shtetls and in many towns, were caught between two fires: "If the rock falls on the clay pitcher, or if the pitcher falls on the rock—woe unto the pitcher!"

My father had made up his mind that the family would remain in Vienna, where all three sons would attend the university and practice their professions. All we needed was peace; everything else would take care of itself. We were sitting around the table, the "cigarette factory." We had to fill hundreds of thousands of hulls with mostly inferior, dusty tobacco. This time everyone held his tongue. Each of us thought there was no going back, and that it was probably for the best. Our old homeland would become foreign, but what if the new homeland remained foreign for us?

We drank a final glass of tea before going to bed. Looking at my mother, my father said: "We old folks just have to hold out until you three no longer need us." We children should have contradicted them, but none of us spoke a word.

People were pouring into the center of Vienna from everywhere, singly and in small or large groups. I watched the growing clusters walking, almost running across the bridges of the Danube Canal.

I am unable to remember whether I really knew what it was all about and what was going to happen. No one needed to ask directions, they seemed to be following the natural course, which carries brooks into rivers and guides rivers through many twists and turns into the sea. We, the masses in which I found myself, arrived at the Parliament Building too late. As we reached the Kaisergarten, we heard a few shots. Then we sighted a flag, the flag of the republic. Someone said people, Bolsheviks, had tried to run up a blood-red flag, but that had been prevented. Supposedly someone, a Socialist leader, was giving a speech, up on the parliament ramp, but we couldn't hear him.

"November 12, 1918, that's a historic date, the children will learn it in school; it will never be forgotten," a man declared proudly. He looked starved, as if he hadn't eaten for days. Someone replied, "Well, we haven't noticed anything about this historic date over here. And soon it's gonna start raining." We waited for about half an hour, but nothing happened. Then we could sense that the crowd was loosening up, moving. I was among those who were shoved across Ballhausplatz, past the Minorite Church, and into Herrengasse. I paused for an instant on Michaelerplatz, gazing at the façade of the Hofburg. Naturally, nothing had changed. I tried to hide my disappointment from myself. What kind of historic date was that anyway, what kind of revolution? Was it over before it had even begun?

Moving circuitously, through small, deserted streets, I headed toward the office of Hashomer. I found no one there from the group, only two tall girls who were listening to a young man crooning a sentimental Russian song while accompanying himself on the mandolin. They looked at me amazed. I remarked, probably with a nasty expression on my face, "The revolution's broken out, and here, here they're playing the mandolin!" All three of them laughed merrily, as if I had cracked a joke. I hesitated, then joined in the laughter. I remained for a while. They resumed singing.

I sang along for one stanza. Then I took off again.

At home there was almost nothing to eat. Everyone knew that the republic had been proclaimed, and they also talked about the Red Guard, which had supposedly tried to occupy parliament but been driven away without much effort. My parents acted as if the revolution were no special event since the war had ended several days earlier, and the monarchy had fallen. In Vienna, people spoke worriedly, then with deep grief, about Victor Adler. It was rumored that he had died suddenly. On the day of his triumph, his tired heart had stopped beating. People repeated this as if quoting a newspaper article. They found bombastic words of praise to commemorate the labor leader, a middle-class scion who had donated his inheritance to the movement. Granted, he had drifted very far from Judaism, people admitted regretfully. But he had remained an exemplary Jew in a higher sense: true to the idea of justice, he had always obeyed the dictates of his conscience. The loss was all the greater, all the more tragic, because Victor Adler had died on the very day on which we could begin to construct a just and peaceful society.

I took part in that conversation. I reminded the others of Fritz Adler, who was free and who would certainly be at the head of the movement. The conversation was interrupted by the appearance of a soldier, a distant relative, who had been missing in action for some time. During those days and the following weeks, several people who had been thought dead kept turning up. Most of them, seriously wounded, had been imprisoned by the enemy, and now nearly all of them were coming back as cripples.

I left the house to visit Grimme-Langer. When I reached his "staff chancelry," a very long, much too narrow room, I found Chaskel. Everything he wore on his body seemed to have been born with him and to be run-of-the-mill at once. He said Krakowiak would be back right away—Ulrich had just gone out to find me because they needed me. He was sleeping here in the chancelry, but only for a few more days, Chaskel said, for he was going home to his village. Not only because of his parents and the rest of his family, but because he wanted to marry. And he already knew who she was.

Soon Grimme-Langer showed up, followed by two soldiers wearing red cockades. He said gruffly, "You should have come earlier."

He added somewhat more mildly, "In a few hours, let's say one or two days, the revolution will begin, the real one—and *we're* going to fight it. I'll explain later. And now listen, you have to perform a difficult job. *Now, immediately.*"

His companions had sat down at a table consisting of two planks across stacks of old valises. They brought me several notes containing the same text: "Convocation! All-Out Alert!" And underneath, the date: November 13, 6:30 A.M., and the place: a side section of South Terminal. The back of each slip had a family name, usually no first name, and a precise address, floor, and apartment number.

Pointing to the soldiers, Grimme explained that they were Red Guards who could be counted on. That was important, for there was a risk that certain people might take over the Guard and use it for their own purposes. They therefore had to have all good men solidly together. I was to notify the comrades listed on the slips. The others would do the same, but he would stay here. As soon as everyone was alerted, I was to come back, and he would explain everything to me carefully.

I tried to make it clear once and for all that I would do nothing until I knew precisely what kind of politics they were practicing, with whom, against whom. Besides, it was very late in the evening, too late for a boy like me to disturb people who didn't know me and whom I didn't know. Grimme said I should get going precisely because it was so late, and the front doors would soon be locked. I shouldn't lose any time; I should take care of everything and come back fast. He would then explain everything convincingly. He thrust the slips into my coat pocket and walked me to the stairs. I arranged the slips; there were nine. Most of the comrades lived in buildings between Taborstrasse and Praterstrasse. I had to find my way up unlit stairways, which I was used to. But once I reached the landing, I had to strike a match to find the apartment door and the bell.

Even today, as I write and think back to those one and a half hours, I feel depressed and despondent. People always reacted to my ring or knock, but only five doors were opened. Each tenant sent me away gruffly, even nastily. It was usually a female voice, grumpily asking what I wanted and then claiming that the man no longer lived there or didn't want to have anything to do with it all, or that the whole thing was a mistake, I had the name wrong, I was a moron.

Of the people who did open their doors, only one allowed me across the threshold. A very young man in a nightshirt and longjohns. He said, "Langer may be a fine gentleman, but he's a jerk. He talks and talks, and never lets anyone else get a word in edgewise. That's why he thinks he's got people in his pocket. The Red Guard'll fall apart as soon as people find something better. And in any case, they don't like Langer. He doesn't even know what he wants. He doesn't like Socialists, he doesn't like Bosheviks. Throw away the slips, go home, have a good night's sleep, and forget the whole thing. You're still too young, you've got your whole life ahead of you. Here, have a piece of chocolate, let it melt slowly in your mouth, it'll last longer." He shook my hand and said good night.

At another apartment, the door was opened by a fat woman, who shined a flashlight on my face. She took the slip from my hand, read it slowly, spelled it out, then focused the light on my face again, and declared, "Tell the commissar who sent you that the war's lasted long enough. Any woman in her right mind would rather tie her husband to her bed than let him out to be killed!"

Only one man, with a bandaged head and with one eye shut, thanked me cordially and promised to report punctually.

When I had done everything and was walking back to the "staff chancelry," I felt so tired that I could have collapsed on the sidewalk, I closed my eyes, and expected nothing, nothing more. At the same time, I was absolutely certain I had acted like the biggest fool. I couldn't come up with even one sensible reason for getting involved with that pathetic one-armed man, that political muddlehead to whom nothing attached me. I decided to jettison the whole thing, go home, and never forget or forgive my stupidity. But the "chancelry" was on my way. I wanted to tell Grimme how unsuccessful my errand had been and what my opinion was. I found Chaskel at the building entrance. He had been waiting for me, he said. I didn't need to go upstairs. Everything was over. People had come from the workers' and soldiers' councils to arrest Krakowiak, that is, take him away, maybe kill him somewhere. He had defended himself and suffered a hemorrhage. The strangers had run off instantly. Ulrich had summoned the first lieutenant's mother; she had brought him to some sanatorium in the ninth Bezirk. Chaskel handed me a slip of paper with the address of the sanatorium. But I didn't want to take it, I didn't even want to look at it. He said: "Maybe you're right. But me, I'm crying, for he's the best person in the world, he was the best person in the world for me." Chaskel sobbed loudly. I didn't know how to comfort him. I wished him a good trip and went home.

"What happened to you?" my mother asked. She placed her hand on my forehead. "Where are you coming from?"

"From Hashomer," I lied. She called my father. Both of them gazed at me thoughtfully. They told me to get right into bed, drink a hot tea, and swallow an aspirin. I did what they told me to do, hardly saying a word, for I feared my voice might betray my consternation.

Naturally, I felt sorry for Grimme because of his immense loneliness, his confusion, and his diseased lung. But for now, I was terribly disappointed with myself. While my parents talked away at me, I kept looking for a satisfactory explanation for my behavior. Why had I gone to see Grimme that evening? Why had I given in even though I considered his talk drivel? I felt as if people could tell just by looking at me that I had clambered up dark stairways of strange, wretched buildings, hunting for people in order to bring them a message that meant nothing to them and was in any case as unwelcome as the messenger who bothered them late in the evening.

Finally, my parents left me alone. Lying on my couch, I picked up one black volume, then another, but I couldn't read. The room was smoky. I stood up and opened the window. Cold, damp air poured in. I was freezing, but I counted to ten very slowly, then to ten once more, closed the window and crawled back under the blanket, pulling it up to my chin in order to get warm faster. I had to cough. I tried to stifle it, but it got worse and worse.

My mother came in again, gazed at me for a long time, and then averted her face, saying,

"The cough will pass soon, the important thing is that you're home. You see, Ulrich came here again tonight, as soon as you were gone."

"Ulrich? Again? What do you mean?"

"He was here several times—under various pretexts, mainly to mooch. He's some sly chatterbox, your Ulrich!"

"He's not mine! Besides, I'm surprised—"

"Don't be surprised. Keep your arms under the blanket. You shouldn't have opened the window. Don't be surprised. He followed you once and found out where you live. He already knew your name, but he wanted to know more. Tonight, he came to get you, as he was ordered to do, but also to warn you. Why did you get involved with an officer? Isn't Hashomer enough for you?"

"Hashomer is enough for me, but I did get involved with First Lieutenant Grimme or whatever his name may be. And the worst part of it is that I just don't know why."

"And that's why you're so unhappy?"

"Yes. It's horrible not understanding oneself."

After a while she said: "There are the stupidities of the stupid, but intelligent people do just as many foolish things. They're just a little different, but not very different. So don't worry, things like this happen to everyone."

"No, not everyone—and it shouldn't have happened to me!"

"Why not you? Do you have special protection from God? Who isn't protected by Him?"

I wanted to explain to her that God was not the issue, nor was it some stupidity. The only thing that mattered was that a human being must understand his actions and know why he does or does not do something. I began to expound on this, but broke off and lapsed into silence.

She went into the kitchen, got some cough syrup, and gave me two tablespoonsful. Then, quite abruptly, she began telling me about her childhood. After her parents' divorce, she had stayed with her father, who instantly remarried. When she was about three, he strictly forbade her ever to see her mother, my Bobe Feygy, greet her even from a distance, or talk to her again. But Bobe Feygy waited behind building doors and at street corners, remained with her for two or three minutes, talked to her, kissed her, and then vanished. The child had to lie to her father and her stepmother, claiming she hadn't seen her mother, and they punished her for it. Bobe Feygy found out and was unhappy. She bitterly lamented the injustice done to her and her daughter, but would not forgo those encounters, which couldn't possibly be kept secret. She should have exercised restraint and patience and waited until later, when no one could prevent the two of them from seeing one another as much as they wanted to and stand by one another in front of all the world—which is what happened eventually. Eventually. . . . But meanwhile Bobe Feygy and her ex-husband made their daughter's life a hell.

"Why did she do that, such an intelligent woman?" my mother asked. And in her eyes, I saw the small, round tears of a child. I couldn't stand seeing her cry and I turned away.

What's this all about, I wondered, shaken by her distant suffering but unable to see any connection between my behavior and that of Bobe Feygy when she was young.

"After my operation, when my mother was here, the two of us spoke about that time, about my fears and the cruelty of the separation. It hurt us both to think about it, but we also laughed. Especially about the uselessness of all efforts to alienate me from my mother."

I still didn't see any connection between my errands that night and the experiences of a divorced woman. But while my mother, who had pulled herself together, spoke unsentimentally about her past, I suddenly realized that nothing so terrible had happened to me. My submissiveness to Grimme, that sick fool, may have been inexplicable, something I could barely own up to, something ridiculous. But it was no *komedye*.

My mother felt my forehead again, stood up, and said as she left, "You don't have a fever. But don't go to school tomorrow. Stay home. Hashomer will also have to get along without you for one day. . . . Father doesn't want to tell you, but he's hurt, because he feels Hashomer is taking you away from us. And maybe you were drawn to that war invalid

only because you don't want to get away from us, but from your comrades. . . . But why? Where to? To politics? It'll wait for you. Believe me,
it'll wait. And you, you have to learn how to wait, too."

I never followed her advice, for I believed that the time of waiting
had ended and that the new time of fulfillment was dawning.